LLYFRGELL COLEG MENAI LIBRARY
BANGOR
GWYNEDD LL57 2TP
01248 - 370125 / 383329

Return on or befo

599-6.

B/Rus.

John Ruskin

D0673714

SUTTON POCKET BIOGRAPHIES

Series Editor C.S. Nicholls

Highly readable brief lives of those who have played a significant part in history, and whose contributions still influence contemporary culture.

SUTTON POCKET BIOGRAPHIES

John Ruskin

FRANCIS O'GORMAN

SUTTON PUBLISHING

LLYFRGELL COLEG MENAI LIBRARY

First published in 1999 by
Sutton Publishing Limited · Phoenix Mill
Thrupp · Stroud · Gloucestershire · GL5 2BU

Copyright © Francis O'Gorman, 1999

All rights reserved. No part of this publication may be
reproduced, stored in a retrieval system, or transmitted, in
any form, or by any means, electronic, mechanical,
photocopying, recording or otherwise, without the prior
permission of the publisher and copyright holder.

Francis O'Gorman has asserted the moral right to be
identified as the author of this work.

British Library Cataloguing in Publication Data

A catalogue record for this book is available from the British
Library

ISBN 0-7509-2142-0

 ALAN SUTTON™ and SUTTON™ are the
trade marks of Sutton Publishing Limited

Typeset in 13/18 pt Perpetua.
Typesetting and origination by
Sutton Publishing Limited.
Printed in Great Britain by
The Guernsey Press Company Limited,
Guernsey, Channel Islands.

'For the rest, I ate and drank, and slept, loved, and hated, like another'

Ruskin, 'Of Kings' Treasuries' (1864)

ST NO	0750921420
ACC NO	047346
CLASS	B/RUS
DATE	09:05:01
STAFF	SJW

PIRVS

CONTENTS

047346

ACKNOWLEDGEMENTS

It is a pleasure to thank friends and colleagues past and present who have, in many ways, helped me with work on Ruskin. Helen Barr, Dinah Birch, Elleke Boehmer, Daniel Bone, Sandie Byrne, Elizabeth Clarke, Simon Dentith, Robert Hewison, Elisabeth Jay, Juliet John, Alison Kitson, Steven Matthews, Anthony Mellors, Helen Moore, Clare Morgan, Lynda Mugglestone, Clare Palmer, Clare Pettitt, Fiona Robertson, Corinne Saunders, Helen Small, Eric and Mary Stanley, Matthew Stiff, Katherine Turner, Angeli Vaid, Julia Wahnsiedler, Michael Wheeler and Peter Widdowson in particular. Thanks to my brother Chris and my parents for their continued interest and support. This book has profited from the careful reading and advice of James S. Dearden and Catherine Dille: I am grateful. Remaining errors and infelicities are mine.

This book is for Kathie Adare and Clark Lawlor, with love.

CHRONOLOGY

1819   **8 February**. Born at 54 Hunter Street, Brunswick Square

1823   Family moves to Herne Hill

1829   'Derwent Water' published in *Spiritual Times*

1830   Family tour of Lake District

1832   Receives copy of Samuel Rogers's *Italy*

1834   Begins attending Thomas Dale's school

1837   Goes up to Christ Church, Oxford

1839   Wins Newdigate Prize

1840   Temporarily withdraws from Oxford due to illness; embarks on a long continental journey until June 1841

1841   At Leamington writes *The King of the Golden River* for Effie Gray

1842   Takes BA; dates his conversion to naturalism in art

1843   *Modern Painters* I published; takes MA

1845   Unaccompanied by parents, sees tomb of Ilaria in Lucca; is appalled by building work in Venice; visits Scuola di San Rocco

1846   *Modern Painters* II published

1848   **10 April**. Marries Effie Gray

1849   *The Seven Lamps of Architecture* published; with Effie in Venice (until March 1850)

1851   *The Stones of Venice* I published; with Effie in Venice again; marriage under serious strain; learns of Turner's death

1853   Millais paints Ruskin at Glenfinlas; *The Stones of Venice* II and III published

Chronology

1854 Annulment of marriage; Oxford Museum project begins

1856 *Modern Painters* III and IV published

1858 Dates final loss of Evangelical faith; meets Rose La Touche; works on Turner Bequest

1859 Visits Winnington Hall School for first time

1860 *Modern Painters* V published; *Unto this Last* published

1862 La Touches forbid him to meet Rose

1864 **March**. John James Ruskin dies

1865 *Sesame and Lilies* published

1866 **January**. Proposes marriage to Rose; she responds inconclusively

1869 *The Queen of the Air* published; elected Slade Professor of Fine Art at Oxford

1871 Starts *Fors Clavigera*; seriously ill at Matlock; **December**. Margaret Ruskin dies

1874 Hinksey Road project

1875 **25 May**. Rose La Touche dies aged twenty-seven; interest in spiritualism revives; *Mornings in Florence, Proserpina* and *Deucalion* are begun

1877 Whistler sues him for libel over July *Fors*

1878 **February–April**. Serious mental illness; legal constitution of Guild of St George; Whistler trial

1880 *Fiction, Fair and Foul* is published; *The Bible of Amiens* is begun

1884 *The Storm-Cloud of the Nineteenth Century* published

1885 Resigns professorship; begins *Praeterita*

1888 Last continental journey, collapses in Paris

1889 Writes last chapter of *Praeterita*; withdraws permanently to Brantwood, Coniston

1900 **20 January**. Dies of influenza aged eighty; buried in Coniston churchyard

RUSKIN'S EUROPE

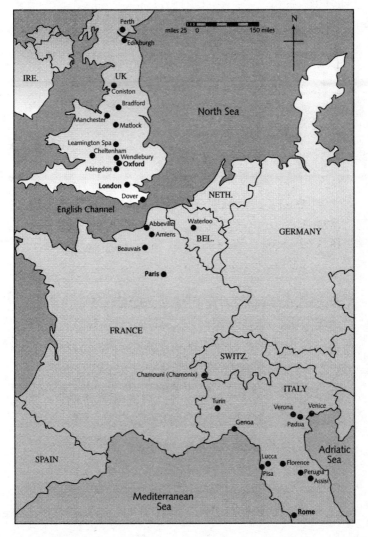

'THIS BOOK SEEMS TO GIVE ME EYES', 1819–43

John Ruskin is England's greatest writer on European visual arts and architecture. He writes luminously about paintings and buildings with a power and passion unmatched by any other English author. He is a social critic of seminal importance whose ideas influenced both his own age and ours. Among other things, he is also an educationalist, architect of the welfare state, literary critic, historian, theologian, scientist, student of Greek myth, watercolourist, autobiographer, university professor and a practical builder of roads. His life is closely linked with some of the most stirring and beautiful places in Europe, such as the Alps, the English Lakes and the city Ruskin called the 'ghost upon the sands of the sea',[1] Venice, though it is also a life, as this book will show, of intense personal anguish and disappointment. What Ruskin so triumphantly accomplished, he achieved often by overcoming pain and disillusionment. He is a great and compelling writer and, though he left no children behind him, he fathered many books, and they continue to live, vividly, and to exert a powerful and enduring influence on those who read them today.

On 8 February 1819, John Ruskin, the only child of Margaret (née Cock) and John James Ruskin, was born at 54 Hunter Street, Brunswick Square, London, a terraced, blank-faced and now demolished house near the present site of St Pancras station. His father, John James (1785–1864), the son of a financially misfortunate Edinburgh merchant, was a highly successful sherry importer (Buckingham Palace would buy directly from him on occasions) whose prudence, enterprise and flair secured a large and increasing income for his wife and son. John James's death in 1864 would leave his son a very rich man. His wife, Margaret (1781–1871), was a committed Evangelical Christian and she brought her son up to share her strong beliefs. But the household was not a puritan one: how could it have been when it depended on John James's discriminating palate? Good food and wine were enjoyed there. Ruskin, a child of precocious mental power, learned to read at an early age, and his parents separately provided him with courses of reading which, in their different ways, profoundly influenced his future life.

At about the time that the family moved, in 1823, to Herne Hill, Ruskin's mother began to make her son read aloud from beginning to end the whole of the Bible, starting all over again at Genesis the day after he had finished the Revelation. This continual reading and rereading was maintained till Ruskin went up to Oxford. It left an indelible impression on his mind and his prose style and, long after he had shed his own Evangelical beliefs, the cadences and vocabulary of the King James Bible permeated his writing. John James Ruskin was more widely read and his enthusiasms – for Shakespeare, Homer and Byron, for instance – also became his child's. But his chief literary legacy to his son was his passion for Sir Walter Scott, whose novels and poems were to provide Ruskin with a lifetime's inspiration and pleasure and a powerful ideal of chivalric conduct.

LLYFRGELL COLEG MENAI LIBRARY

John James's work necessitated a good deal of cross-country travel in search of business, and he took his son with him as soon as he could. From 1824, they began to visit English country houses in pursuit of custom. In 1825, John James took his child further afield to France and Belgium, where they saw the field of the Battle of Waterloo. Even from the earliest, John could not travel without writing down what he saw and thought, or sketching the views before him. Some of his writing was in verse, and his 'Derwent Water' was published in the *Spiritual Times* in August 1829 when he was only ten; it is his first published work.

The family's 1830 tour of the Lake District, travelling via Oxford, Birmingham and Matlock, was recorded in a comprehensive diary, as well as, later, in an amusing but rather pompous poem in rhyming couplets, *Iteriad or Three Weeks Among the Lakes*.[2] The diary, published only in 1990, reveals the young Ruskin's already highly developed facility for close observation and preserving fine details of what he saw. His long account of Gloucester Cathedral, with which he concluded his narration of the family's travels, was the beginning of a lifetime's literary labour in fastidiously recording the architecture and monuments of great historical buildings.[3]

A gift in 1832, for his thirteenth birthday, of a copy of Samuel Rogers's somewhat mundane poems *Italy* was a significant event for the young Ruskin, though not because of the poetry. *Italy* in its 1830 edition contained illustrations by Prout, Stothard and, chiefly, Joseph Mallord William Turner, perhaps the first time Ruskin had seen the work of the artist whose name was to become inseparable from his. (He may have seen a Turner oil at Appuldurcombe when he visited the Isle of Wight in 1828.) Ruskin later met Rogers and embarrassingly praised the quality of the illustrations, omitting to compliment the poet on the poetry. But he knew what he thought more important.

In 1833, the Ruskins were abroad again, this time more ambitiously. They took an extended continental tour into mainland Europe that included Strasburg, Schaffhausen, Milan, Genoa and Turin, and their son began his acquaintance with one of the most influential landscapes of his life, the Alps. 'How shall I thank you for carrying me again over the summits of the higher Alps[?]' Ruskin wrote to his father on their return: 'Mamma says you are

LLYFRGELL COLEG MENAI LIBRARY

spoiling me. I say I am spoiling, despoiling, and taking the spoil of your pocket [. . .] What a dear Papa, I've got'.[4] Later, in his autobiography, Ruskin said the first sight of the Alps was 'not only the revelation of the beauty of the earth, but the opening of the first page of its volume'.[5] During this tour, Ruskin, while in Paris, met Adèle Domecq, the young daughter of one of his father's business partners; he later developed a youthful passion for her which lasted some years and caused him to be gravely distressed emotionally. Margaret Ruskin was appalled by her Catholicism.

In 1834, the fifteen-year-old Ruskin published his first work in prose, an essay on the colour of the waters of the Rhine in Loudon's popular *Magazine of Natural History*. It revealed further his gift for careful visual study, and was an early sign of his fascination with science which would form another important facet of the adult Ruskin's interests. It was his greatest ambition as a child, he recalled in *Deucalion*, not to be a famous artist or a famous writer, but the president of the Geological Society.

Ruskin was initially educated by his mother, although he was also visited by a number of private tutors. From the middle of 1834 to December 1836, he attended a small school run by the progressive, Evangelical clergyman Thomas Dale. 'Mr Dale crams them [Ruskin's fellow students] & me/Beyond the bounds of our digestion',[6] Ruskin wrote in verse to his father in February 1835. One of his essays surviving from Dale's school, solemnly titled 'Does the Perusal of Works of Fiction Act Favourably or Unfavourably on the Moral Character?', was a piece about the merits of Sir Walter Scott and it indicated something of the influence that John James had from such an early age on the taste and opinions of his son. Ruskin also took drawing lessons from Charles Runciman, and later from Copley Fielding and James Duffield Harding. Ruskin was highly gifted from the first and well able to imitate the picturesque style demanded of him.

In 1836, Ruskin attended lectures on the new academic subject of English literature at King's College, London – Robert Browning was also briefly there. In January 1837, a month before his eighteenth birthday, he went up to the aristocratic but run-down Christ Church, Oxford (beer was stored in the chapel which also was, and is, Oxford's cathedral). His father, always concerned with matters of social status, had ensured his son's position as a gentleman commoner, a distinction which carried some kudos among the under-graduates. Ruskin's parents hoped he would impress at Oxford both socially and academically and then take Holy Orders. But the reality of university was duller than Ruskin had expected. The dead hand of the unreformed Oxford syllabus lay heavily on him at Christ Church, though he found one tutor, the Revd Walter Lucas Brown, more interesting than the rest, and kept up a long and querulous correspondence with him for years after they had both left the college. He also met and made friends with the industrious, ambitious Henry Acland, later to become Regius Professor of Medicine at Oxford, a man who would play a significant part in Ruskin's life.

Fortunately, writing college essays did not take up all of Ruskin's time, and he managed to publish the articles comprising the *Poetry of Architecture* in the *Architectural Magazine*, 1837–8. These were important in setting out early thoughts, to be developed in *The Seven Lamps of Architecture* and *The Stones of Venice*, on the relationship between architecture and national character and moral temper. They were also an opportunity for Ruskin to castigate the condition of much English building, 'disgraced by every variety of abomination'[7] he said, and an utter lack of 'unity of feeling, [which is] the basis of all grace, the essence of all beauty'.[8] In due course, he would begin to recommend how this situation could be improved. Ruskin also won the University's prestigious Newdigate Prize for poetry in 1839 – at his third attempt – with the dutiful offering of *Salsette and Elephanta*. Arthur Hugh Clough came second. It was the most successful Ruskin's polished, elegant but conventional poetry was to be.

Illness suddenly intervened in Ruskin's Oxford career. Perhaps his mother had feared it would, for she stayed in Oxford in lodgings on the High Street throughout her son's residence there and he took tea with her more or less daily. In April 1840, he coughed blood, a disturbing suggestion of consumption, and was temporarily withdrawn from the University. A long continental tour was suggested as a remedy, and on 25 September the family departed on the journey that would take Ruskin to many of the major centres of Italian art and architecture. Travelling comfortably and in style to Genoa, Lucca, Pisa and Florence, the Ruskins reached Rome at the end of November 1840. The information gathered on this long tour, during which the family also stayed at Naples, Sorrento and Amalfi, was fundamental to the writing of Ruskin's first major work, *Modern Painters* I (1843). On 6 May 1841, the family reached Venice (they had visited it for the first time in 1835, when Ruskin wrote mock-Byronic poetry about it). 'Thank God I am here!' Ruskin wrote enthusiastically in his diary: 'it is the Paradise of cities [. . .] I am happier than I have been these five years – so happy – happier than in all probability I ever shall be again in my life'.[9] He was often given to such hyperbole, but he was also more seriously convinced that present happiness was always fragile.

Back in England in June 1841, Ruskin was still ill, and he tried the grim salt-water cure of the well-known maverick Dr Henry Jephson of Leamington. It seemed, against the odds, to work. While in Leamington, Ruskin took up his pen to write his only work of fiction. He said in *Praeterita* that he was utterly 'incapable of acting a part, or telling a tale'.[10] But *The King of the Golden River* was proof otherwise. A morality tale about justice and generosity in the imaginary land of Stiria, Ruskin wrote it, he said, 'solely for [the] amusement' of a 'very young lady'.[11] She was his future wife, Euphemia Chalmers Gray (he sometimes called her Phemy, but she was mostly known as Effie), who had first stayed with the Ruskins on her way to school in August 1840 and then, on her way back in July 1841, had challenged him to write a fairy tale. In 1850, John James arranged for *The King of the Golden River* to be published, with illustrations by Richard Doyle, and it has remained a popular children's story.

Ruskin, later in 1841 and feeling stronger, was determined to return to Oxford to finish his degree, though his long absence precluded the possibility of a high class. In April 1842, he duly sat the papers – he came to hate the whole notion of competitive exams and believed their educational value to be nonexistent – and was awarded an honorary double fourth, the highest the examiners could give him under the circumstances. While sitting his exams, his mother wrote to him sternly of his duty: 'believe me John you never will know *permanent* happiness in this world ever if you do not seek it in promoting the happiness of others and in Loving and obeying your God'.[12] But Ruskin was increasingly sure he would not serve God by entering the Church. A visit to Walter Lucas Brown, by this time rector of the unremarkable village of Wendlebury near Oxford, and living a dull life of sermons and sick visits, cannot have done much to persuade him of the Church's attractions.

The year 1842 also saw a change in Ruskin's thinking about art and his practice as an artist. Trained by his own drawing masters in the picturesque mode, he underwent a conversion to naturalism. That year, Ruskin remembered much later in his autobiography, he had been drawing 'a bit of ivy round a thorn stem' on the way to Norwood when he perceived suddenly that 'I had virtually lost all my time since I was twelve years old, because no one had ever told me to draw what was really there!'[13] Later, the message was reinforced by another incident. While trying to draw a 'small aspen tree against the blue sky',[14] Ruskin saw again the importance of representing nature truthfully. 'With wonder increasing', he wrote, '[. . .] I saw that [the branches] "composed" themselves, by finer laws than any known to men.

At last, the tree was there, and everything that I had thought before about trees, nowhere.'[15] The stories may well be inventions (Ruskin's diary of 1842 does not confirm them), designed to give clearer shape to a gradual process. But the fact is that Ruskin threw off the picturesque mode in favour of naturalism, and began to think about fidelity to natural truth in great art more carefully. His reflections on this and on the role of the imagination were given public expression in *Modern Painters* I.

Back in October 1836, the Revd John Eagles had published an essay in *Blackwood's Magazine* scornfully reviewing Turner's newly exhibited *Juliet and her Nurse* (controversially relocating Juliet from Verona to Venice), *Rome from Mount Aventine* and *Mercury and Argus*: 'perfectly childish', Eagles said of this last: 'All blood and chalk'.[16] Ruskin was incensed and drafted a response. But his father thought it should be shown to Turner himself, who was discouraging (he did not take any interest in criticism, he said), and it was not published until 1903. The manuscript essay, however, was the seed of the first volume of *Modern Painters*, and the beginning of Ruskin's lifelong championship of Turner.

The last months of 1842 and first of 1843 found Ruskin hard at work on this book, developing the conceptions sketched in the manuscript reply to Eagles and bringing together ideas on naturalism and the imagination with thoughts prompted by the Italian art he had seen on his 1840–1 continental journey. In the middle of writing there was a disturbance: the Ruskins moved house, to 163 Denmark Hill, a large three-storey town house in the part of London then known as the 'Belgravia of the South', set in 7 acres of land and close to Dulwich with its important picture gallery. It was a sign of John James's increasing success as a businessman.

Modern Painters I was published in May 1843 by Smith, Elder and Company. Ruskin did not use his own name, calling himself simply 'a Graduate of Oxford'; like many pseudonyms, it did not secure anonymity for long. *Modern Painters* I, a landmark achievement that established new terms for English art criticism, was not a book with a single line of argument: it was an interwoven texture of Christian theology, aesthetics, philosophy, art history and polemic. But chiefly Ruskin endeavoured to explicate in stirring prose Turner's paintings to an audience that had so far proved unable to comprehend them, and in doing so to lay out the foundation of a whole theory of art and perception. Turner was a landscape artist of exceptional power, Ruskin said, whose paintings showed a grasp of natural fact fused with emotion, and revealed an imagination capable of entering the essence of natural form. He was, Ruskin wrote, 'the only painter who has ever drawn a mountain, or a stone'.[17]

Reviews were slow, but eminent readers were not. Charlotte Brontë told her publisher, 'Hitherto I have only had instinct to guide me in judging of art; I feel now as if I had been walking blindfold – this book seems to give me eyes'.[18] Tennyson, concerned about money, wanted to borrow a copy. Other hearty expressions of admiration followed and Ruskin was quickly invited into the refined and glittering social circles of the London literary and artistic world as his name and fame spread. His father was delighted.

When the formal reviews did come, they were predictably mixed for such a ground-breaking book. George Darley in the *Athenaeum* remarked on the volume's 'great acuteness amid still greater blindness',[19] but Walt Whitman said that any artist would find it 'invaluable'.[20] The most critical review was, unsurprisingly, from John Eagles. His long essay in *Blackwood's* for October 1843 spoke of the 'palpably fulsome, nonsensical praise'[21] of Turner, and denounced Ruskin as 'for the most part extremely unintelligible'.[22] It would not be the last time that Ruskin prompted a censorious response from the press. But this time it was of little concern. Ruskin, reassured by his devoted father, knew that he had embarked on a work which mattered.

T W O

'THE GHOST UPON THE SANDS OF THE SEA', 1844–54

Following the publication of *Modern Painters* I, Ruskin for a time went through bouts of intense work followed by periods of what looked like determined work avoidance. He tried to write a preface to the second edition but felt despondent about it, and took consolation in dining out and attending other society events including his first private view at the Royal Academy. In May 1844, however, he joined his parents on another continental journey which provided him with a greater focus. The reviving tour was chiefly to Chamonix and the Simplon, and gave Ruskin opportunity to acquire further geological knowledge of the Alps which would be put to good use in volume IV of *Modern Painters* and in *Deucalion* in the 1870s.

While in an Alpine inn, Ruskin met a 'severe-looking, and pale, English (as we supposed) traveller'[1] who turned out to be James Forbes, the eminent Scottish geologist and author of *Travels Through the Alps of Savoy* (1843). He was a man with a romantic appeal for Ruskin, always drawn to history and ancestry, for he was the son of the first woman Sir Walter Scott had loved, Williamina Belches Stuart. In the 1870s, Ruskin would defend Forbes's integrity as a scientist against derogatory claims from one of the most high-profile of mid-Victorian natural philosophers, John Tyndall. It was partly Ruskin's way of defending Scott and the heroic ideal he stood for against the modern world.

On the way back from the Alps, where Ruskin had been assiduously reading Dante's *Divine Comedy* in Cary's translation, he spent time in the Louvre, extending his knowledge of Italian painters, especially Tintoretto, Titian, Perugino and Veronese. But he was disappointed, for he wanted to see the paintings in their original locations and not so awkwardly displayed in Paris. Returning home, he lost his focus again. 'Have not written a word since my return from Chamounix,' he wrote in his diary on 20 October, 'for my days pass monotonously now.'[2]

Ruskin did manage to read, however, and also studied Turner's *Liber Studiorum* carefully, but he was not at ease. Eventually, he decided that the second volume of *Modern Painters* could not be written without a further visit to Italy, a compensation for his disappointment in Paris. And this time, at the age of twenty-six, he would go without his parents. His mother made her presence felt as best she could, however, by secretly packing the Evangelical favourite John Bunyan's *Grace Abounding to the Chief of Sinners* in his bag as an antidote to Romish Italy and as a way of keeping her son firmly in the Protestant fold. By early May 1845, Ruskin was in Lucca studying the medieval art and architecture with which he would become increasingly preoccupied. Here he saw, in the north transept of the cathedral, Jacobo della Quercia's serene tomb of Ilaria di Caretto, which he described as his 'ideal of Christian sculpture',[3] saying it was 'in every way perfect: truth itself, but truth selected with inconceivable refinement of feeling'.[4]

The tomb would exercise a potent influence over him until his last days, and would become one of the female forms, together with Carpaccio's St Ursula, he associated with Rose La Touche after her death.

Ruskin saw the work of other artists too, including Giotto, Antonio Veneziana and Orcagna: he was absorbed and wrote energetically to his father about his discoveries. In Pisa, he was overawed by the Campo Santo and the work of the *quattrocento*. Looking at the decoration of the cathedral doors, he declared: 'It is the most wonderful thing I ever saw'.[5] More dispiritingly, he also saw precious works of art decaying, or their destruction in the name of 'restoration'. Ruskin accepted the need for 'preservation', but deplored any other interference.

Ruskin then moved on to Florence to see the Fra Angelicos in San Marco, and more Giotto and Ghirlandajo; he also visited Como, Macugnaga and Verona. By the second week of September, he was back in the 'Paradise of cities', Venice. But this time his response was different. He was appalled, in a 'state of torment',[6] by the 'improvements', the laying of gas pipes, which necessitated the destruction of bridges over the rios, the restorations and the plain neglect. The Palazzo Ducale was being whitewashed. And the new railway bridge from Mestre had been built: Wagner was so delighted when he crossed it that he threw his hat into the sea; Ruskin was aghast. The sight of a remaining fragment of Giorgione's frescoes on the Fondaco dei Tedeschi was a melancholy symbol of how many precious things had gone from Venice. 'I was never so violently affected in all my life', he wrote, 'by anything not immediately relating to myself [. . .] Venice is lost to me'.[7]

But in the Scuola di San Rocco Ruskin found the dramatic paintings by Tintoretto that immediately overwhelmed him. 'I have had a draught of pictures today', he wrote to his father on 24 September, 'enough to drown me. I never was so utterly crushed to the earth before any human intellect as I was today, before Tintoret.'[8] In *Praeterita*, Ruskin associated his discovery of San Rocco with the beginning of *The Stones of Venice*, saying that 'Tintoret swept me away at once into the "mare maggiore" of the schools of painting which crowned the power and perished in the fall of Venice; so forcing me into the study of the history of Venice herself'.[9] It was characteristic of Ruskin to describe his own life in such a way, speaking of being 'swept into' an interest and 'forced' into a study: he understood himself as directed by external circumstances and profoundly obedient to duty. Tintoretto's champion he became, nonetheless, and remained so.

Returning home via Beauvais, Ruskin was determined to complete *Modern Painters* II, and was hard at work on it until the end of March 1846. It was published in April, as Ruskin was beginning his next European journey. *Modern Painters* II, the most theoretical and philosophical of the five volumes of *Modern Painters*, was also the most overtly Christian in its linking of aesthetic truth with divine law. It was an attempt to demonstrate the nature of the quality of beauty, explain the operation of the imagination as a power which 'reaches truths by no other faculty discoverable'[10] and introduce to an English audience the then almost unknown religious art of Fra Angelico in Florence and, remembering the Scuola di San Rocco, the 'various stupendous developments of the imagination of Tintoret'.[11] This time his efforts were greeted enthusiastically. The 'most valuable contribution towards a proper view of painting, its purpose and means, that has come within our knowledge', said the *Foreign Quarterly Review*.[12]

The month after this success, Ruskin had reached Venice again. There were some signs of unease between himself and his father, who had accompanied him on this visit, not least because John James still had hopes that his son would make a name for himself as a poet, not as a prose writer. The tensions would grow and the gap between father and son become wider. The disquiet was partly over the young woman for whom Ruskin had written *The King of the Golden River* and who was on his mind increasingly now: Effie Gray. In the first few months of 1847, Ruskin and Effie's relationship became closer. 'She is so good-natured and open, graceful and really rather pretty',[13] he had written in 1843; now he was becoming more seriously attracted. Probably in the middle of October 1847 they became engaged.

Effie was a pretty, chatty, vivacious young woman whose ambitions were chiefly social: she was happiest in the soirées, balls, concerts and dinner parties that filled the days of mid-nineteenth-century high society. She was intelligent, witty and not short of admirers; she wanted from life what it was usual for a woman in her social position to want. But she was about to marry the wrong man.

Ruskin's letters after his engagement reveal him troubled, sometimes very anxious, though they are full of declarations of love for Effie. They married on 10 April 1848 in the drawing room of Effie's family home in Perth and spent their first night at Blair Atholl. But there was no love making, and there never would be. Quite why this was has never been clear. Ruskin, who always privately denied any suggestion of impotence, later claimed there was something unpleasant about Effie's body. Given he had never, of course, seen a naked woman in the flesh before, perhaps he was shocked by the difference between the idealized forms he had seen in art and Effie's real body. It seems unlikely, though it is the most usual explanation. Ruskin later implied that he did not see anything more of her than her shoulders and breasts. For whatever reason, the marriage got off to a bad start.

Parental expectation and plain interference would make matters worse. Effie, enjoying a 'continual round of festivities'[14] in the first months of her marriage, quickly became irritated by the over-anxious care of Ruskin's parents: 'they talk', she wrote, 'constantly to him about what he ought to do, and in the morning Mrs. Ruskin begins with "don't sit near these towels John they're damp"'.[15] It must have been gruelling. John and Effie's honeymoon was delayed by revolutions in continental Europe and Ruskin busied himself reading theology, writing to Walter Lucas Brown about it, and 'looking at France longingly'.[16] But in August, four months after their marriage, they set off for a busy eleven weeks, chiefly in Normandy, where Ruskin studied the Gothic architecture of Northern France intently.

Ruskin's work was shortly to result in a further highly influential book, *The Seven Lamps of Architecture* (1849), which he was writing after his return from the Continent in the house at 31 Park Street that the affluent and generous John James had secured for his son and daughter-in-law. Not that this house provided much independence from the older Ruskins, who expected the couple, or, better still, John alone, at Denmark Hill frequently. Relations between Effie and Ruskin's parents were declining quickly and in the last months of 1848 and first of 1849, she was under strain and, as she would frequently be, physically unwell.

In April 1849, Effie was too ill to join her husband and his parents on their next major continental tour, which provided Ruskin with material for the next two volumes of *Modern Painters*. While they were away, *The Seven Lamps* was published. Ruskin here discussed the Gothic warmly, and his arguments would have a significant impact on the development of Victorian architecture. Making a provocative distinction between architecture and mere building, Ruskin analysed the Gothic in reverently Christian terms under the seven headings: sacrifice, truth, power, beauty, life, memory and obedience. For many an aspiring Gothic Revivalist, *The Seven Lamps* became standard reading, and the call for massiveness and colourful polychromy in new building was particularly influential.

Ruskin was pleased with the appearance of *The Seven Lamps*, but, far away in the Alps, he was preoccupied with the contrast between the sublime scenery of the mountains and the terrible poverty and sickness of the Alpine peasants. In church at Sallanches in June he was horrified to see men who 'were all ugly, diseased or stupid', many suffering 'goitre and cretinism'.[17] He reflected on the significance of this disagreeable contrast for a long time. He wrote affectionately to Effie, but also suffered a period of depression, 'one of my low fits',[18] in early August after what he called 'very painful self examination'.[19]

Effie, left at home, wanted to go away herself, and in particular to Venice about which her husband had talked so much; returning to London from Switzerland, he promptly agreed to take her. Reaching the city in November, they settled for their long visit at the luxurious Hotel Danieli: Ruskin straightaway visited the major buildings to reassure himself that they had not been destroyed by the Austrian army which now occupied the city. He studied the Ca' d'Oro in detail, and immersed himself in drawing and note-taking throughout the city, balancing precariously on ledges on the Palazzo Ducale to obtain better views of the window tracery: 'most singular in every way'.[20] He was providing himself with an unparalleled resource of journals and sketchbooks for writing *The Stones*, though it was 'hard, dry, mechanical toil',[21] he said later, and his father thought it a waste of his powers.

Meanwhile, Effie enjoyed a sparkling social life in elevated Venetian circles, sometimes in the company of Charles Paulizza, an appealingly romantic Austrian first lieutenant. The Ruskins left on 9 March 1850, and immediately after arriving home John commenced an inflexible work routine to complete the first volume of *The Stones*. 'I am permitted', he wrote piously in his diary on 23 April, as soon as he returned to London, 'to continue this volume after a happy sojourn of more than a year abroad: thanks be to God.'[22] Later, he would add of the whole project, 'May God help me to finish it to His glory, and man's good.'[23] Writing continued into the first months of 1851: it was engrossing. It was also, of course, solitary. Effie, alone, contrived to turn London to her advantage and to enjoy as busy a social life as she had in Venice.

The first volume of *The Stones of Venice* was published on 3 March 1851: Ruskin was thirty-two. It was the first of three volumes which, when complete, would stand together with *Modern Painters* as Ruskin's most powerful achievement in the fields of art and architecture. Volume I commenced with a sonorous warning making it clear that Ruskin was talking not only of Venice of the past, but of England today. A trinity of great sea powers, Ruskin wrote, Tyre, Venice and England, were known to human history: 'Of the First [. . .] only the memory remains; of the Second, the ruin; the Third, which inherits their greatness, if it forget their example, may be led through prouder eminence to less pitied destruction'.[24]

During the course of the three volumes, Ruskin told how Venice rose to prosperity in the thirteenth and fourteenth centuries as a Christian sea-trading power, a city of justice, reverence and order. The city's moral and spiritual health was reflected in the glories of its painters and the sacred splendour of its Gothic architecture, which was the style not only of its civic buildings but also of the ordinary domestic dwellings of the merchants. Corruption, injustice and the decline of true Christian faith, Ruskin continued, began to take hold at the beginning of the fifteenth century and, the contagion gradually spreading, it was revealed in the art and architecture of the Venetian Renaissance. The deplored productions of the Renaissance signified for Ruskin the true state of post-Gothic Venice's moral and spiritual ill health: art honoured the human not the divine, it was sensual, preposterous, grotesque, arrogant. It was, at its nadir, the 'manifestation of insolent atheism'.[25]

The central chapter of the second volume, 'The Nature of Gothic', was the most frequently anthologized and immediately influential section. Here, Ruskin described how Gothic ornament was the natural expression of the joy of the labourer, content in his work. It was 'one of the very few necessary and inevitable utterances of the century', said William Morris later, and it 'seemed to point out a new road on which the world should travel'.[26]

Ruskin was hard at work on the second volume as soon as the first appeared, though in May 1851 he found time to write some letters to *The Times* defending the work of the early Pre-Raphaelite painters Millais and Holman Hunt exhibited in the Royal Academy that year. Ruskin's name would always be associated, though not without some confusion, with the principles of the Brotherhood thereafter, especially in view of their commitment to naturalism.

Mr and Mrs Gray, Effie's parents, visited London in the summer to see the Great Exhibition, begun in May 1851, but Effie was anxious to be in Venice once more. In early August, she and her husband set off and reached the city for their second extended visit at the beginning of September where they learned sadly of Paulizza's death. Again, it was a time of immense work for Ruskin as he gathered more material for the completion of *The Stones*. He studied architecture intensively, sending occasional samples of his writing to John James in London for approval. He was convinced that the Palazzo Ducale would soon be destroyed and that he must record its features in every detail. He was especially concerned with the carvings of the capitals.

On 28 December, he learnt of the death of Turner, 'my earthly Master'.[27] It was not unexpected, but a blow nonetheless. With rather indecent haste, he wrote to his father immediately telling him what pictures to acquire: 'Buy *mountains*, and *buy cheap* and you cannot do wrong.'[28] He would later discover he had been made an executor of Turner's will, a position which would bring him endless problems.

In March 1852, Ruskin, still hard at work on his Venice project, wrote some letters to *The Times* on the Corn Laws, but his father dissuaded him from publishing them. The event was significant for two reasons. First, it showed Ruskin's increasing interest in controversial political issues; second, it revealed that this interest would meet with little approval from John James, who thought that his son was moving dangerously away from the work in which he would achieve lasting fame. Tension between father and son over politics increased significantly in future years and proved to be a source of acute anxiety for both of them.

Problems were also becoming apparent, as Margaret Ruskin had feared when she packed Bunyan in her son's luggage, with Ruskin's Evangelical faith. 'You speak', Ruskin had written to his Christ Church friend, Henry Acland, in May 1851, 'of the Flimsiness of your own faith. Mine, which was never strong, is being beaten into mere gold leaf'.[29] The doubts continued. Diary entries and letters in 1852 indicated growing spiritual unease and restless questioning of the literalism of Evangelical belief.

As for the marriage, Effie and Ruskin had been living largely independent lives in Venice: Effie had continued the hectic pace of socializing; Ruskin had been hard at work. On their return to London in July, he continued his isolation, spending large portions of his day in the study at Denmark Hill, away from his wife. By the end of the year, while he was still deeply absorbed in completing the remaining two volumes of *The Stones*, Effie's health was collapsing. She was seriously unwell, both physically and mentally.

By Easter of the following year, 1853, things had become even worse, and the Gray family were at odds with the Ruskins over their daughter's well-being. In the summer in Scotland with her husband for a holiday, Effie's friendship with the painter John Everett Millais, for whose *Order of Release* she had already sat, became closer. Possibly on the day that *The Stones of Venice* volume II was published, Millais began his famous portrait of Ruskin at Glenfinlas, a *tour de force* of Pre-Raphaelite realism. But perhaps even as he painted, Millais was falling in love with his subject's wife.

The final volume of *The Stones* was published in October; in November, Ruskin delivered the *Lectures on Architecture and Painting* in Edinburgh, and the first part of his *Giotto and his Works in Padua* appeared at the end of the year. 'I do not know,' Ruskin said, 'in the annals of art, such another example of happy, practical, unerring, and benevolent power' as Giotto's.[30] But if work continued, it was clear that the marriage could not. In April 1854, Ruskin was served a Suit of Nullity by Effie's lawyer, seeking annulment on the grounds of non-consummation. In July, it was granted. Ruskin made no reference to the annulment in his diary. He was away in

Chamonix as it was pronounced, relieved to be amid the sublime beauties of the natural world. 'Thank God, here once more', he wrote on his arrival on 10 July, 'and feeling it more deeply than ever. I have been up to my stone upon the Bréven, all unchanged, and happy.'[31]

THREE

'THE SUM OF TWENTY YEARS OF THOUGHT', 1855–9

Freed from the necessity of having to attend social events with Effie, Ruskin, after the annulment of his marriage, became much more sociable. His correspondence grew, and new friends and acquaintances dined at Denmark Hill where Ruskin now returned to recommence a familiar life in close proximity to his parents. At the end of 1854, he spent time in Oxford with Acland, who was eager to enlist Ruskin's services in a major new University development. Acland wanted to build a University museum which would be a centre of science teaching, containing lecture rooms and research laboratories as well as exhibition space. It was part of his ambitious plans, much resisted in certain academic quarters, to improve the provision for science at Oxford, a university still largely dedicated to providing a classical and mathematical education.

In November 1854, Ruskin involved himself directly in another educational project by agreeing to take practical drawing classes at the recently opened Working Men's College in London, founded by a group of Christian Socialists, F.J. Furnivall, Charles Kingsley and F.D. Maurice. Furnivall, an inveterate former of societies, provided an early meeting to discuss the College with a reprint of Ruskin's 'The Nature of Gothic' chapter from *The Stones*, calling it *On the Nature of Gothic Architecture* and adding a subtitle: *And Herein of the True Functions of the Workman in Art*. It was an indication of the role that chapter was playing in the growth of Victorian socialist thinking.

Much of 1855 passed in writing volumes III and IV of *Modern Painters*, and in meeting more friends. Eminent men and women of letters, including the chief representatives of the new generation of poets, Robert and Elizabeth Browning, Alfred Tennyson and Coventry Patmore, became Ruskin's acquaintances; he kept a shelf of his bookcase especially for the new verse he was reading. His friendship with the painter and poet Dante Gabriel Rossetti and the beautiful but distraught Lizzie Siddall became closer. *The Harbours of England* was published this year too, a description of Turner's sequence of drawings of the same name and a kind of long prose poem of Ruskin's enchantment with the sea. He also began to issue *Academy Notes*, his commentary on new paintings in the Royal Academy. This he would do until 1859, with an isolated final issue in 1875.

Work on Acland's museum gathered pace in 1855. Ruskin, at his friend's request, suggested principles of decoration for the building, commented on aspects of the overall design and even came down to lecture the masons on the site. Both he and his father gave money to help fund its construction. Ruskin invested much, financially and intellectually, in the museum because he saw it as an ideal opportunity to test out practically some of the claims he had made in 'The Nature of Gothic': he wanted a great new Gothic building for Victorian England, richly decorated with natural forms, carved by workers not slavishly following rigid plans but creatively inspired by the spirit of the

Gothic itself. The museum was to be, Ruskin thought, a temple to natural history and the careful and reverently Christian study of God's creation, as well as solid evidence that, under the right conditions, Victorian Britain could build its own Gothic and thereby proclaim its moral and spiritual health.

The year 1856 saw continued work on the museum, as well as Ruskin's penultimate trip in the company of his parents to the Continent, chiefly to Switzerland. During the trip he renewed his acquaintance with the Harvard art historian, Charles Eliot Norton, who, though much more liberal-minded than Ruskin, was to become a good friend and correspondent. The third and fourth volumes of *Modern Painters* were published in 1856 also. Ruskin had created the appearance of contradiction by praising as great art, in volume I, that which displayed in abundance accurate and detailed knowledge of the natural world yet approving so warmly the religious, human-centred art of Giotto, Tintoretto and Fra Angelico in volume II. In volume III, he attempted to solve this by dividing 'the art of Christian times into two great masses – Symbolic and Imitative',[1] declaring that accurate representation of the natural world was relevant only for the latter.

Ruskin also pursued the task begun in *Modern Painters* I of defining, without oppressively fixed and inflexible rules of the sort advanced by Sir Joshua Reynolds, the nature of greatness in art. Ruskin said in volume III that great art could only be produced by moral and spiritually healthy men who sincerely loved noble and beautiful subjects, and were able imaginatively to penetrate into their essence. 'Great art', Ruskin wrote, 'is precisely that which never was, nor will be taught, it is pre-eminently and finally the expression of the spirits of great men'.[2]

Modern Painters IV, published in April 1856, displayed the results of some of Ruskin's geological study in the Alps, and also returned to the original subject of landscape painting. Concerned with the accuracy of mountain representation, he provided extensive, rather dry, geological information about the structure and formation of the Alpine range. He also, more engagingly, discussed the influence of mountains on the moral and spiritual temper of those who lived in their midst. In the chapter 'The Mountain Gloom', he wrote down some of his thinking about the impoverished and unhealthy

Alpine peasants who had so troubled him in 1849, speculating on the place of evil in a divinely created world. 'We cannot know the reason of these things', he wrote, 'but this I know – and this may by all men be known – that no good or lovely thing exists in this world without its correspondent darkness'.[3]

Ruskin's Alpine study grew out of an intense love of mountain form, the 'beginning and the end of all natural scenery', he said.[4] Volume IV was at its most memorable when Ruskin described the influence of mountains not on people in general, but on himself. The 'slightest rise and fall in the road,' he declared, '– a mossy bank at the side of a crag of chalk, with brambles at its brow, overhanging it, – a ripple over three or four stones in the stream by the bridge, – above all, a wild bit of ferny ground under a fir or two, looking as if, possibly, one might see a hill if one got to the other side of the trees, will instantly give me intense delight, because the shadow, or the hope, of the hills, is in them'.[5]

Ruskin had returned from the continental tour at the end of September 1856, noting irritably that it had left him unrefreshed. Swiftly, however, he immersed himself in Turner work, writing to Prime Minister Palmerston in December explaining his willingness to catalogue the huge, largely unknown archive of the artist's drawings and sketches left to the nation on his death. Ruskin's first approach to the National Gallery, making the same offer, had been ignored, but he was convinced that his unique knowledge of the painter's work was required for the proper ordering and cataloguing of the collection.

In January 1857 Ruskin's *Notes on the Turner Gallery at Marlborough House* was published, his briefest Turner publication. It concluded with his bravura explication of the *Fighting Téméraire*: 'of all pictures of subjects not visibly involving human pain, this is, I believe, the most pathetic that was ever painted', he said.[6] Thereafter, until the summer, Ruskin was hard at work with the Turner drawings and sketches. In June, *The Elements of Drawing* came out: it partly comprised material prepared for the drawing classes at the Working Men's College, where Ruskin continued to teach. 'I can promise you', he said, 'that an hour's practice a day for six months [. . .] will give you sufficient power of drawing faithfully whatever you want to draw'.[7]

Further evidence of Ruskin's growing concern with politics and economics appeared in 1857.

Inspired by the Great Exhibition, the corporation of
Manchester had decided to mount an Art Treasures
exhibition which would display some 'of the most
precious and remarkable works of Art in the United
Kingdom'.[8] As part of their programme, they invited
Ruskin, the leading art critic of the day, to speak. In
July 1857, Ruskin rented a farmhouse in Cowley,
outside Oxford, to write the two lectures he would
give. They were first called *The Political Economy of Art*
but later published as *A Joy for Ever*. The lectures
featured a pointed and unKeatsian subtitle '(*and its
Price in the Market*)' – Keats's 'A thing of beauty is a
joy forever' was a line written in gold over the
central exhibition space in Manchester.

The lectures were the most extended public
excursion into politics that Ruskin had yet made.
He developed his argument that it is only in a just,
well-ordered society that art can properly flourish;
he declared that art was thus an index of a nation's
well-being, and also that England had forgotten that
truly enriching wealth was not money but virtue.
Remembering too the destruction and neglect of
art he had seen abroad, he told his listeners that
they had a direct duty to buy fine works from the
Continent to prevent their ruin. The audience

received the lectures with enthusiasm. John James, however, called them 'meddling with Political Economy',[9] though was reassured that his son had not spent too much time on them. The *Manchester Examiner and Times*, anticipating the more general hostility from the press towards Ruskin's political work, lamented that the two lectures – important trial pieces for *Unto this Last* (1860) – showed 'what genius can become when divorced from common sense'.[10]

Back in London in October after a brief period in Scotland, Ruskin was soon occupied with cataloguing, mounting and putting into order the Turner drawings: 'upwards of nineteen thousand pieces of paper', he was amazed to find.[11] Some of this laborious work, in which he was helped by George Allen, his assistant, brought disturbing surprises as Ruskin discovered to what extent Turner, like his other great hero Walter Scott, had declined in the later years of his life. The painter gradually became, Ruskin wrote regretfully to his father, 'encumbered with sensuality – suspicion – pride – vain regrets – hopelessness – languor – and all kinds of darkness and oppression of heart',[12] and this degeneration was increasingly manifested in his drawing. Many, Ruskin thought, could never be exhibited.

Most of all, Ruskin was horrified to find drawings of what he called a grossly obscene kind, dreadful evidence of the degenerate 'sensuality' of Turner's mind. Ruskin, with the agreement of the National Gallery, saw that these pornographic drawings were burned. Writing the preface to *Modern Painters* V in 1860, Ruskin remarked that he had 'never in my life felt so much exhausted'[13] as when this Turner work was over, which it was, finally, in May 1858. He had brought great learning to the task and learned more than he brought.

That same month Ruskin began what was meant to be a restorative holiday abroad, if the term 'holiday' can ever be applied to his travels. He went to Switzerland and then to Turin, where he spent a fortnight in careful study of Paolo Veronese's *The Presentation of the Queen of Sheba*, a picture of 'quite inestimable value', he wrote later in the last volume of *Modern Painters*.[14] While studying it, he was shocked, he wrote in his diary, by the fact that 'I never saw one person pause to look at it.' However, 'at least four out of five stopped with evident interest, and not a few with expressions of sincere and energetic admiration, before [a picture by] Canaletto', an artist Ruskin particularly loathed.[15]

In 1877 in *Fors Clavigera*, the series of political letters he began to publish in 1871 and which included much auto-biography, Ruskin remembered that Veronese's 'inestimable' painting played a key role in the final crash of his long-troubled Evangelical faith in 1858. The 'crisis of the whole turn of my thoughts', he wrote in *Fors* for April 1877, 'being one Sunday morning, at Turin, when, from before Paul Veronese's Queen of Sheba, and under quite overwhelmed sense of his God-given power, I went away to a Waldensian chapel where a little squeaking idiot was preaching to an audience of seventeen old women and three louts, that they were the only children of God in Turin; and that [. . .] all the people in the world out of sight of Monte Viso, would be damned. I came out of the chapel, in sum of twenty years of thought, a conclusively *un*-converted man'.[16] This is almost certainly another retrospectively tidied-up account, adding an artificially neat end to a long process of doubt which Ruskin had been experiencing for some years. But certainly, from about this time, Ruskin was finally freed from the Evangelical doctrines he had inherited from his mother.

The year 1858 was consequential for Ruskin in another way too. It was the occasion of his first meeting – 'The Beginning of Sorrows', he wrote mournfully later[17] – with the girl who would come to dominate and profoundly disturb his life: Rose La Touche. He met her first with her mother Maria and sister Emily in their house on Great Cumberland Street in London. Rose was ten; Ruskin thirty-nine. Mrs La Touche, a minor Irish novelist and poet from a cultured background, was hoping that Ruskin might advise her on her daughters' education in painting and drawing. Ruskin, entranced by Rose, agreed, to her mother's amazement, to teach her himself. Emotionally vulnerable anyway, he gradually fell in love with Rose, a charming but disturbed girl who grew into an unbalanced young woman, preoccupied with her spiritual salvation and, alas, it seems, dangerously anorexic. A few months after Ruskin's first meeting with Rose, Mrs Ruskin sent her fruit and a copy of *The King of the Golden River*. Given its original dedicatee (Effie), it would prove an ironic gift.

Early in 1859, Ruskin made the acquaintance of some other young girls who were to make a more enduringly positive impression on him. Delivering the lecture 'The Unity of Art' in Manchester in

February 1859, a few days after his fortieth birthday, Ruskin observed Margaret Alexis Bell and five of her pupils in the audience. Bell was Headmistress of Winnington Hall School for girls near Northwich in Cheshire. She was a person of strong character who drew admiration from students and visitors to the school alike. Georgiana Burne-Jones, wife of the painter, called her 'an extremely clever woman of a powerful and masterful turn of mind'.[18] Her school was innovative and broad-minded as it offered sports, painting, needlework, dancing and music, alongside traditional subjects such as natural history, history, mathematics and Bible classes. There was a strong culture of authority – 'Absolute submission to their Principal was expected and given', said Mrs Burne-Jones[19] – and also an open-minded but sincere regard for Christianity. Bell was disillusioned with the Methodism with which she had grown up and attracted to the Broad Church movement; her own wrestle with a faith inherited from her family drew Ruskin to her. The tolerant but reverent attitudes she fostered in her progressive school also seemed to him a healthy alternative to the oppressive doctrines of Evangelical Protestantism.

At Miss Bell's invitation, he visited Winnington in March 1859. 'I have learned & heard a great deal that has been useful to me', he wrote afterwards to his father.[20] Thereafter, he visited more, and corresponded prolifically with individual girls, the girls collectively and with Miss Bell herself. His association with Winnington gave him direction after the loss of his faith, and encouraged him to reflect more deeply on the nature and aims of proper education, and on girls' education in particular.

Ruskin's involvement in the University museum in Oxford had been continuing on and off throughout this whole period, but it was proving a source of irritation. The trouble was partly over the decoration, external and internal, of the building. Ruskin was determined that the façade, in accordance with the principles of 'The Nature of Gothic', should be abundantly decorated with inspiring, instructive natural forms: 'simple life, and richly bestowed public joy', he called it.[21] But getting what he wanted past the University authorities, and from the stone carvers themselves, proved troublesome. Money was also a problem: the museum was costing more than the University was prepared to pay. In December 1858, Ruskin had been so annoyed with the obstacles thrown in his path, especially the trouble made by the masons and architects, that he had fired off a letter to his incurably gossipy friend Lady Trevelyan saying: 'I've done with architecture and won't be answerable for any more of it. I can't get the architects to understand its first principles & I'm sick of them'.[22] Visiting in January 1859, he observed crossly that the coloured parts of the decoration were simply 'vile'.[23] He was disenchanted; the ambitions he had for the museum were disappointed.

It was all the more ironic, as Robert Hewison points out with truly Ruskinian hyperbole, that the Oxford Museum, in which Ruskin believed God's creation would be reverently and sincerely studied, was 'the site [in 1860] of a famous confrontation that blighted the paradiasical garden of Natural Theology for ever'.[24] This confrontation was one the most famous moments in the history of Victorian science. The biologist and controversialist T.H. Huxley and Samuel Wilberforce, Bishop of Oxford, met in the museum in July 1860 to debate the deeply divisive theories of evolution following the publication of Darwin's *Origin of Species* in 1859.

It was a debate that Huxley was widely acknowledged to have won and emblematic of the growing divorce in Victorian England between the orthodox assumptions of Natural Theology and the claims of modern empirical science. It was an ironic twist in the story of Ruskin and the museum. But it was not the last. The museum would make another vexing appearance in Ruskin's life some years after he had returned to Oxford, partly at Acland's instigation, as the first Slade Professor of Fine Art.

Beyond the problems of the museum and the new, heartening interest in Winnington, Ruskin was busy with other projects in 1859. On 10 May, he published *The Two Paths*, a collection of five separate lectures delivered in London, Manchester, Bradford and Tunbridge Wells, but each one aiming, he said, to illustrate a single principle: the 'dependence of all noble design, in any kind, on the sculpture or painting of Organic Form'. This, he declared, was 'the vital law' lying 'at the root of all that I have ever tried to teach respecting architecture or any other art'.[25] Later in May, he and his parents set out on what was to be their final family tour. It was to Germany, principally to see the Titians held in collections there, and, again, to Switzerland. Ruskin

William Bell Scott, Dante Gabriel Rossetti and John Ruskin in Rossetti's garden, 1863. (By courtesy of the National Portrait Gallery, London)

John James Ruskin, Ruskin's father, *c.* 1863. (The Ruskin Foundation [Ruskin Library, University of Lancaster])

Margaret Ruskin, Ruskin's mother, by James Northcote (oil on canvas), 1825. The painting is in the dining room at Brantwood. (The Ruskin Foundation [Ruskin Library, University of Lancaster])

Effie Ruskin by John Everett Millais, 1853. This portrait was painted for John Ruskin at Glenfinlas. (National Trust Photographic Library/Derrick E. Witty/Wightwick Manor, Wolverhampton, The Mander Collection [The National Trust])

The north-west porch of San Marco, Venice, *c.* 1850. This is a daguerrotype from John Ruskin's collection and shows the image reversed. (The Ruskin Foundation [Ruskin Library, University of Lancaster])

The rear of Denmark Hill, Ruskin's London home. (The Ruskin Foundation [Ruskin Library, University of Lancaster])

An undated photograph of Rose La Touche with water-colour decoration of wild roses. (Reproduced by courtesy of the Director and University Librarian, the John Rylands University Library of Manchester)

Brantwood, Coniston, 1999. Ruskin retired here permanently towards the end of his life.(Photograph courtesy of Brantwood Trust, Coniston)

A portrait of John Ruskin by Elliot & Fry, London, 1865. (Private Collection/The Stapleton Collection/Bridgeman Art Library, London/New York)

John Ruskin, self-portrait with blue neckcloth, *c.* 1873. (The Pierpont Morgan Library/Art Resource, NY)

John Ruskin's pencil drawing with water colour of the north-west porch of San Marco, Venice, 1877. After completing this drawing, Ruskin wrote '. . . left as the colour dried in the spring mornings of 1877'. (The Ruskin Foundation [Ruskin Library, University of Lancaster])

John Ruskin's copy of
St Ursula's head, a detail from
Carpaccio's *The Dream of
St Ursula*. (Private Collection)

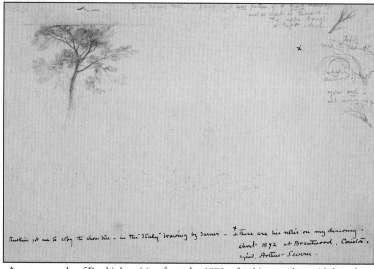

A rare example of Ruskin's writing from the 1890s after his complete withdrawal to
Brantwood. This page contains Ruskin's firmly written comments on a copy by
Arthur Severn of a tree by Turner. (Courtesy of Wolverhampton Art Gallery, England)

was not knowledgeable about German art itself, and he had been sorely embarrassed when forced to admit as much to the National Gallery Site Commission in 1857, especially as Dean Milman, a friend of Effie's, was present.

But Effie, who had married Millais shortly after the annulment of her marriage to Ruskin (she did not find true happiness with him either)[26] belonged to a part of his life that was now over. In any case, Ruskin would never think of the end of his marriage as particularly significant. However, he would later describe 1859 as the year preceding a momentous change in the direction of his intellectual energy and literary work. He would say that 1860 was the most significant turning point of his writing career, and the beginning of his proper work.

LLYFRGELL COLEG MENAI LIBRARY

FOUR

'FRIGHTFULLY TORMENTED IN VARIOUS WAYS', 1860–8

While Slade Professor at Oxford, Ruskin always enjoyed dramatic gestures. In the lecture theatre he would flap his MA gown like a giant, menacing bird; he would paint swirling clouds of polluted air over glass placed on a Turner landscape to illustrate industrial society's effect on the natural world. His students went sometimes just to see the spectacle. In 1877, witnessed by his later editor and biographer Edward Tyas Cook, he delivered a lecture in which a dramatic gesture memorably enforced a point about his own life. Standing before his undergraduates, Ruskin had beside him the five, large, sumptuously bound volumes of *Modern Painters*; in his hand he held a small copy, in faded green cloth, of *Unto this Last*. Pushing the volumes of *Modern Painters* away from him as he spoke, Ruskin, as Cook recalled it, declared: "'in the summer of 1860, and in the valley of Chamouni [*sic*] I gave up my art-work and wrote this little book" (taking it up in his hand) – "the beginning of the days of reprobation [. . . and] the central work of my life"'.[1] Ruskin, distancing himself from the product of seventeen years of writing on art, was neatly describing his life as divided into two, as a career in which art wholly gave way, with the completion of *Unto this Last*, to social issues, politics and economics.

The year 1860 was certainly very important, but it did not quite mark the dramatic division in his life's work that Ruskin claimed. Beyond his forty-first birthday, he did not 'give up' art work. He wrote widely on painting, sculpture and engraving, developing new areas of interest and new fields of expertise. But he rarely wrote again with such intense passion and emotion about art; seldom now would he deploy the awesome powers of his rhetoric to communicate vividly what he saw on canvas or in stone. After 1860, he wrote more about social issues, and his energies became devoted increasingly to schemes of social improvement, to thinking and writing on industrial society, education and citizenship, the ideal community, the proper nature of government, the dignity of labour. Interest in such concerns can be traced back to *The Stones of Venice* with its underlying concern with the health of society. But now he would aspire more actively to prevent England from following Venice's path to ruin.

Symbolically, then, the final volume of *Modern Painters* was published in 1860. The first volume had come out in 1843; seventeen years later, on 14 June 1860, the final part appeared. *Modern Painters* V was chiefly concerned with the law of organic unity and its importance in pictorial composition, especially in the work of Turner. The great work of art is a unified whole, Ruskin wrote, just as the 'highest and first law of the universe – and the other name of life, is [. . .] "help" '.[2] This principle of cooperation was a key theme of the political economy of *Unto this Last* and Ruskin's social criticism in general; it was a major point of correspondence between his understanding of the nature of great art and his conception of healthy society.

Presaging the gloom that Ruskin would come to feel about society in general, *Modern Painters* V was also a lament. He felt that recent history showed how greatness, godliness, truth, beauty and human nobility had rarely been recognized by less gifted men and women. In particular, he wrote, the nineteenth century 'has caused every one of its great men, whose hearts were kindest, and whose spirits most perceptive of the work of God, to die without hope: Scott, Keats, Byron, Shelley, Turner'.[3] It was a melancholy note on which to end this monumental publication.

Ruskin was abroad when *Modern Painters* V was published, and in some emotional turmoil over Rose. But he was also at work on the essays that would comprise *Unto this Last*, the second major publication of 1860. The individual essays were first serially published by the *Cornhill Magazine*, edited by the novelist William Makepeace Thackeray, and they prompted immediate controversy. Indeed, Thackeray, cautious and unwilling to associate his journal with a dispute, stopped their publication after the fourth essay because, as Ruskin put it later, they 'were reprobated in a violent manner, as far as I could hear, by most of the readers they met with'.[4] The viciousness of some of the formal reviews, even given the Victorian press's penchant for caricature and exaggeration, was astonishing. The conservative *Saturday Review*, most notoriously, wrote of the 'utter imbecility of Mr. Ruskin's reasoning powers',[5] of his 'worse than ridiculous'[6] arguments, and concluded Ruskin 'is a perfect paragon of blubbering'.[7] Ruskin had never before met with such vehement public hostility. Feeling emotionally fragile anyway, he sank into a depression, gloomily reflecting on the sudden disapproval of his work.

Reviled at first, *Unto this Last* was eventually to become one of Ruskin's most influential and significant texts. It was a forceful statement against competitive capitalism, challenging the principles of *laissez-faire* economics and the convictions of Ricardo and Adam Smith with a bravura energy and compelling moral strength. Ruskin argued that economics was not a separate, isolated science concerned simply with financial prosperity: it involved all aspects of individual and national life, especially a country's moral well-being. True wealth, he said, was not judged by the sum of a nation's gold, but by the virtue and happiness of its people. And all of this depended on society functioning as an organic whole and obeying the universal law of 'help', defined in *Modern Painters* V.

Cooperation and mutual support is life, Ruskin said: competition and mutual conflict, death. His argument about the true nature of wealth led him to the climax of *Unto this Last*, the keystone of his radical economics: 'THERE IS NO WEALTH BUT LIFE.'[8] They were resonant words repeated in much socialist and reformist literature of the later years of Victoria's reign.

Ruskin did not know that *Unto this Last* would achieve the importance it did. His unhappy mood after the publication of the essays in the *Cornhill Magazine* was not, however, only to do with the reviewers. He was also at the beginning of a prolonged period of malaise over his relationship with Rose La Touche, and the dispiriting story of Ruskin's private life from the publication of *Unto this Last* onwards is one of distress, frustration and sometimes near-despair, only infrequently broken by periods of tranquillity, contentment and hope.

Writing to Margaret Bell on New Year's Eve 1860, Ruskin remarked, 'I have been much depressed & unable to attend to anything myself',[9] telling her in March the following year that 'all things [seem] to me entirely sad'.[10] In February

1861 he described himself to Charles Eliot Norton as having 'no joy in what I do (the utmost I can do being to keep myself from despair about it and do it as I would break stones)'.[11]

One of the problems was Rose's view (and her family's) of Ruskin's heterodox religious opinions. His remaining Christian belief was rapidly deserting him. To Charles Eliot Norton he wrote in August 1861, with a feeling of searing betrayal, that he had been misled by God: 'I looked for another world, and find there is only this, and that is past for me'.[12] He was coming to think of life as an awful and troubling mystery. Looking for consolation, he travelled in the summer to Switzerland, and found some temporary relief in drawing, reading and walking among the mountains he loved. But the year ended with him in a state of distress and confusion again.

Early in 1862, under the shadow of his feelings for Rose and preoccupied with his fractured faith, Ruskin tried to immerse himself in Turner work again, helping to identify and clean some of the drawings in the Turner bequest, many of which were now mouldering and filthy. His view of the fate of great men and their art seemed to be right in this case.

After a visit to Winnington Hall School, his relationship with Rose reached a crisis in April when her parents, unhappy with their daughter's friendship, forbade them to meet for a while. He wrote miserably later to Mrs Cowper: 'since that day of April 1862, I have never had one happy hour, — all my work has been wrecked'.[13] Some modern writers have suggested that Mrs La Touche's hostile attitude towards Ruskin's friendship with her daughter was partly a consequence of the fact she had fallen in love with him herself. There is perhaps some truth in this.

Ruskin's work continued, nonetheless. In June 1862, he published the first of four 'Essays on Political Economy' in *Fraser's Magazine*, edited by J.A. Froude: these would later be published in 1872 as *Munera Pulveris* but only after they had caused Ruskin a good deal of tribulation. In the first instance, his father disapproved. In July, Ruskin felt compelled to write him a strongly worded letter saying the 'one *only* thing you can do for me is to let me follow out my work in my own way and in peace. All interference with me torments me and makes me quite as ill as any amount of work.'[14]

Another problem with *Munera* followed in April 1863, when, in an unwanted repeat of the *Cornhill*

Magazine incident, Froude, under instruction from the publishers of *Fraser's*, refused to accept any more instalments. The critical antagonism over the work that Ruskin later called 'the first accurate analysis of the laws of Political Economy which has been published in England'[15] was too much. Gravely disappointed and feeling his political ideas had now been doubly rejected, Ruskin contemplated living permanently in Switzerland, safely away from his detractors. It was one of his many attempts to find for himself a permanent place of peace and contentment. He also briefly turned to the safer, less controversial subject of geology, lecturing at the Royal Institution about the Alps on 5 June. He could certainly pursue this subject without being assaulted by the press. The lecture was later published as *On the Forms of the Stratified Alps of the Savoy*.

In August, Ruskin was a little more cheered by a positive notice from Philip Hamerton in the *Cornhill* praising *Modern Painters* and its effort to teach the principles of a comprehensive art theory: 'The art article is entirely right and admirable', Ruskin wrote happily to his father on 30 August, '– and pleasant because it puts me into great good-humour with myself'.[16] Hamerton repaired some of the damage the *Cornhill* had done in 1860 and provided Ruskin with a rare optimistic feeling about his work. In October, concern over Rose agonizingly returned: she was psychologically ill, a condition precipitated by feelings of guilt consequent on receiving her first communion without being confirmed. Rose's mental state was always fragile, and she was constantly prey to the most debilitating anxiety.

In December, Ruskin was reflecting on his own unhappiness, and thinking about the overpowering force of his feelings for Rose. He also wrote to his father about his upbringing, complaining, as he would do in *Fors Clavigera* and *Praeterita*, of his parents' treatment of him: 'The two terrific mistakes which Mama and you involuntarily fell into', he said fiercely, 'were [. . .] you fed me effeminately and luxuriously to that extent that I actually now could not travel in rough countries without taking a cook with me! – but you thwarted me in all the earnest fire of passion and life.'[17] He would continue to work through his ambiguous feelings about his childhood to the end.

By the time John James received his son's irritated letter, he had only a few months to live.

Frail and ill, he died of uremic poisoning at the age
of seventy-eight in March 1864. He had lain in his
son's arms throughout the last, pitiful day of his life,
tossing and turning in wretched delirium. Ruskin's
response was complex: he wrote to Acland a few
days after his father's death talking of his 'bitter
regret' for 'the pain I have given him'.[18] However,
in another letter to Acland, he spoke of the 'loss of a
father who would have sacrificed his life for his son,
and yet forced his son to sacrifice his life to him,
and sacrifice it in vain'.[19] One practical thing was
certain however: Ruskin was now a very rich man.
He inherited £120,000, together with substantial
property. The cash inheritance was about £6 million
in today's terms. Ruskin, one of the greatest critics
of capitalist Victorian society, awkwardly owed
much of his freedom to write and think throughout
his life to the commercial success of his father's
highly profitable business.

If financial troubles never plagued him, emotional
distress continued to engulf Ruskin in 1864, as it had
the year before. He was miserably preoccupied with
Rose, now aged sixteen, the worthlessness of his
own work and the shards of his faith. But there was
some important writing done despite this. In April,

the prophetic lecture 'Traffic' was given in Bradford Town Hall, where Ruskin had been invited to advise the city fathers on the architecture of their new stock exchange. Should it be Gothic or was there something better for the building? Asking Ruskin such a question was a mistake, and 'Traffic' began with an affront: 'I do not care about this Exchange, –' Ruskin said bluntly to his audience, 'because *you* don't; and because you know perfectly well I cannot make you.'[20] His listeners must have been amazed. He then delivered a sonorous warning, one of the finest he ever gave, addressed not only to Bradford but the nation: 'Continue to make that forbidden deity [Riches] your principal one,' he declared, 'and soon no more art, no more science, no more pleasure will be possible. Catastrophe will come; or, worse than catastrophe, slow mouldering and withering into Hades.'[21] It was the language of an Old Testament prophet made serviceable for the nineteenth century.

In December 1864, the two highly crafted lectures, 'Of Kings' Treasuries' and 'Of Queens' Gardens', published in 1865 as *Sesame and Lilies*, were delivered at Rusholme Town Hall, near Manchester. *Sesame and Lilies* became Ruskin's most popular book, selling more copies in the nineteenth century than any other of his works. It was a favourite prize in girls' schools, a widely recommended primer of ideal behaviour. In 'Of Kings' Treasuries', Ruskin, in the spirit of 'Traffic', told his audience to seek after true riches not after mere material wealth; in 'Of Queens' Gardens', he discussed 'what special portion or kind of [. . .] authority, arising out of noble education, may rightly be possessed by women'.[22] It was the first of his extended considerations of women's power, and the proper scope of female education. His description of the 'separate characters'[23] of men and women, however unacceptable today, was, in 1864, an eloquent formulation of what was expected of a woman as the maker of the home, and a resonant description of that home itself as 'the place of Peace; the shelter, not only from all injury, but from all terror, doubt, and division'.[24]

The year 1865 would prove a more balanced and calmer year for Ruskin than the previous ones, less convulsed by emotional trauma. The work that commenced in January indicated that Ruskin was regaining some of his spirit and beginning to feel that his labour was not quite the stone-breaking monotony he had earlier described to Charles Eliot Norton. The series of essays called *Cestus of Aglaia*, on the laws of 'Art practice and judgment',[25] was commenced and some planning was done for more geological writing. Little was written in his diary during this time, however, and the occasional letter spoke chiefly of his quiet work. The order and calm of Denmark Hill, one of the idealized models for the 'place of Peace' in 'Of Queen's Gardens', provided Ruskin with a tranquil base from which to write the occasional letter to Winnington, or to Norton or to sketch out a lecture plan. He was hardly filling his days, but he was doing more than he had for some time, and in a better frame of mind.

In December, *The Ethics of the Dust* was published, a series of discussions between an Old Lecturer (Ruskin) and various girls aged between nine and twenty, based on his experiences at Winnington. In *The Ethics*, Ruskin combined accounts of Egyptian myths and descriptions of crystallization with moral teaching, using crystallization as a metaphor for orderly behaviour and dutiful obedience. He found in crystals evidence of a will, a living force in nature, which reached its fulfilment in human life.

'You may [. . .] earnestly believe', the Old Lecturer said to his pupils, 'that the presence of the spirit which culminates in your own life, shows itself in dawning, wherever the dust of the earth begins to assume any orderly and lovely state'.[26] The form of the book – a version of the Socratic dialogue – was innovative for Ruskin, though commonly used by other educational writers, and it marked the beginning of a period of generic experimentation. Carlyle thought *The Ethics* marvellous.

If 1865 had provided some respite from emotional turmoil, 1866 began with an event which plunged Ruskin back into it. It seems – the evidence is not very clear – that about the time of Rose's eighteenth birthday (3 January), Ruskin proposed marriage to her. Certainly, she did not answer immediately but, on 2 February, asked him to wait for three years, when she would be twenty-one and Ruskin a few weeks away from his fiftieth birthday. He would always be haunted by this date. In April, the La Touches left for Ireland: the parents, recanting their former decision, had given their 'reluctant permission'[27] for the relationship to go on, but Ruskin always felt he was in a difficult position with them. He relied on his friends, especially Georgiana Cowper, to maintain his spirits. But 1866, some of which he spent on the Continent, was a dismal year.

The year 1867 was in emotional terms little better, and Ruskin's physical health deteriorated too. He was, he wrote in January, 'Frightfully tormented in various ways'.[28] Some of Ruskin's discomfort was now to do with the directions of his career and writing. Amid the care of his private life, he was also reassessing his public one, thinking through options and pondering what paths his literary career should now take. A letter from Thomas Dixon early in the year happily provided him with a suggestion. Dixon was a skilled craftsman, a cork-cutter from Sunderland, but also interested in art and letters. He was determined, like many a Victorian autodidact, to improve his education by correspondence with great men. Max Müller said he 'showed a clearer insight into the true objects of all my writings [. . .] than many a review'.[29]

Dixon wrote to Ruskin, who was still smarting from his experience with the *Cornhill Magazine* and *Fraser's*, asking for copies of his political economy work, and this gave Ruskin an idea for a new way of expressing his political views: the public letter. Thus began the *Time and Tide* series, addressed to questions 'bearing upon honesty of work, and honesty of exchange'[30] and emphasizing cooperation together with 'just and benignant mastership'.[31]

On Monday 4 May 1868, Ruskin wrote simply 'Peace' in his diary.[32] He did not say what he meant, nor was the word appropriate. The early months of 1868 had been, again, times of terrible mental strain, during which Ruskin had written almost nothing for publication. His correspondence with Mrs Cowper continued frantically, in which he described the complexities and oscillations of his feelings for Rose. Only in his visit to northern France in the late summer and early autumn did he find some opportunity for more positive work and thought, enjoying for 'the moment the quiet investigation of beauty'[33] as he drew Abbeville and its surrounding countryside with some of his old flair and zest for the visual world. By the end of the year, he had begun some botanical work – preparations for *Proserpina* – which would occupy him for the remainder of his active life. As he wrote about the mythological and emotional significance of flowers through history, this work would become one of the ways in which he could unite public teaching with the insistent private themes of love, grief and loss, which, for Ruskin, had dominated so much of the 1860s.

FIVE

'I WILL ENDURE IT NO LONGER QUIETLY', 1869–78

Ruskin was fifty years old on 8 February 1869. 'How utterly sad', he wrote, 'these last birthdays have been, in 67 and 68. I am not much better to-day, but in better element of work.'[1] He was right about the work. During the next few years, he began to find clearer directions in his writing, and new ways of presenting his ideas and communicating with his readers; he was also to realize, in part, that he had fallen in love with an ideal, with someone he had partly imagined. He began to comprehend more of Rose's mental imbalance and to feel vexed and irritated by her. But while he distanced himself sometimes from the real Rose, who died, after long mental illness and gradual physical deterioration, in May 1875 aged only twenty-seven, the ideal she represented never left him. His obsession with Rose took new forms and had further significant consequences for his writing in the 1870s, his last full creative decade. They were years of more fertile thinking and more active literary work than the 1860s, but much of what he published on art, myth, science, politics and society was related, in one way or another, to his complicated feelings for her.

In March 1869, Ruskin lectured at University College London, and South Lambert Art School on mythology, a subject he was becoming more and more interested in. He spoke on 'The Greek Myths of Storm', part of his preparation for *The Queen of the Air*, his book on Greek myths of cloud and storm, which he published in June. Ruskin's renewed interest in myth – he had discussed it in *Modern Painters* V – arose in part as a consequence of his loss of Evangelical faith. Writing on mythology was a way of discussing moral and spiritual issues without speaking about Christianity, of talking about divine power in the world without explicit Christian reference. Myths, Ruskin now thought, were sacred narratives worthy of continual respect in which the ancient world had expressed its reverence for nature, communicated noble moral truths and given shape to its understanding of divine power. Benighted modern society could learn a great deal from them, he argued in *The Queen of the Air*, if it would only study them with 'patience and human sympathy'.[2]

Ruskin, who expected a great deal from his close friends, left Charles Eliot Norton to see *The Queen of the Air* through the press, and departed in May for Verona, chiefly to gather information on tombs there for the Arundel Society. He was enchanted by the countryside also: 'all transcendent,' he wrote of the wild flowers he had seen, 'as if painted by the spirit that painted the hills'.[3] He also went to Venice, the first time he had been there since 1852 with Effie. He was cheered to be back, 'full of good hope',[4] reclaiming the city for himself once more. '[It] is very a dream [*sic*], again, to me, this Venice', he wrote to his mother, '– the fair sea and sky and listless motion – and being able to stop almost at any instant and walk into a place where there are Titians or Bellini's [*sic*] – or Tintorets – one after another – Church after church, and room after room – all precious'.[5] Holman Hunt came for a time too, and Ruskin showed him the Scuola di San Rocco. According to Hunt, Ruskin told him there how little religious faith he had left.

While he was away, important news came. Oxford University had unanimously elected Ruskin the first Slade Professor of Fine Art. He was initially daunted, feeling this was an appointment of considerable responsibility, though part of him relished the opportunity to play a part in undergraduate teaching. Returning to London at the end of August, he settled down to 'gradual preparation for University work'.[6] In October, he wrote to Mrs Cowper saying that he was now resigned with regard to Rose: 'I can never be to her – what I was to her once – Nor she what she was to me',[7] yet he was plagued throughout the last months of the year by troubling dreams. The year ended positively, however, and on 30 December, he wrote elatedly in his diary that he had seen 'The loveliest sunrise – certainly the loveliest thing I ever yet saw in this world.'[8]

On 7 January 1870, Ruskin unexpectedly met Rose, the first time he had seen her in four years, in the Royal Academy: he offered her back some of her letters which he always carried, but she said simply

'No'.[9] He wondered if she had understood what he had meant by this gesture. Over the following weeks, she wrote to him but he was angry, telling her harshly that he would dedicate his Oxford lectures to the woman who had 'taught me/The cruelty of Religion/And the vanity of Trust'.[10] But the lectures were a useful distraction, and he tried to put Rose to the back of his mind as he worked on them.

On his fifty-first birthday, he delivered his Inaugural at Oxford: the crowd was so large the venue had to be moved from the museum to the Sheldonian Theatre where, many years before, Ruskin had recited his prize-winning Newdigate poem. The Inaugural, which reiterated Ruskin's familiar argument that 'The art of any country *is the exponent of its social and political virtues*',[11] ended with a rare pro-imperialist statement: England, he said, 'must found colonies as fast and as far as she is able, formed of her most energetic and worthiest men'.[12] It was an uncharacteristic remark, and perhaps what he felt he ought to say in the august surroundings.

A born lecturer, Ruskin was nervous about his first Oxford appearances. However, looking back in 1887 on his first term's lectures, he realized he was proud of them, calling them nothing less than 'the most important piece of my literary work done with unabated power, best motive, and happiest concurrence of circumstance'.[13] In late May 1870, Ruskin was back in Venice, considering the work of Carpaccio, whom he had discovered a year earlier and described excitedly as a revelation. Carpaccio's paintings, in the Accademia and the Scuola San Giorgio de' Schiavoni, would exert a great influence on him, and become inextricably linked with his feelings for Rose.

Busy in Italy, Ruskin was also busy when he returned: drawing, writing new lectures, entertaining and studying in the British Museum. Mrs La Touche, meanwhile, had been in touch with Effie Millais, trying to find out the truth about Ruskin's alleged sexual problems. Effie, evidently still dreadfully angry, wrote an attack on her former husband in reply: his mind is, she said, 'most inhuman; all that sympathy he expects and gets from the female mind it is impossible for him to return excepting upon artistic subjects which have nothing to do with domestic life'.[14] The sound of real incompatibility was still horribly audible.

Time and Tide had given Ruskin the idea of using the public letter as a platform for his political views.

In January 1871, he developed the idea further, beginning the series entitled *Fors Clavigera: Letters to the Workmen and Labourers of Great Britain. Modern Painters* III had been subtitled 'Of Many Things' and the description would serve *Fors* well too. The letters, which lasted on and off until 1884, contained some of Ruskin's most inventive forms of writing, far-reaching ideas and practical schemes for the regeneration of society, and pungent denunciations of the modern world, its corruption, thoughtlessness, ugliness and irreverence. The *Fors* letters were sometimes quirkily written, containing hundreds of allusive references, approaching themes from unexpected angles, suddenly changing from seriousness to jest to satire, but their moral commitment inspired many readers, including philanthropists and political radicals, in the later years of the nineteenth century.

Through *Fors* Ruskin proposed the formation and constitution of what became known as the Guild of St George, an alternative, communitarian society employing manual labour, which was both hierarchical and cooperative in its organization. Initially suggested in *Fors* in 1871, it took Ruskin, who donated a considerable amount of his own money to the plan, some time to obtain proper legal status for the Guild, which was to be presented in due course with various portions of land. Ruskin's ideas prompted a number of actual experiments in agrarian, communitarian living such as that at Bewdley, in the Wyre Forest. Here, a group of Ruskin enthusiasts from Liverpool formed a successful farming community in August 1889: they were made of 'the stuff of heroic pioneers', one contemporary wrote.[15] The Guild of St George exists still today, a charitable foundation which supports educational work. *Fors* occupied much of Ruskin's time throughout the 1870s: it was nothing less than a one-man political journal, an ambitious, passionate effort to revive the health of the nation and to stimulate political and moral thinking about the condition of England.

Ruskin spent February 1871 at the Crown and Thistle Inn in Abingdon, being driven by carriage into Oxford almost every day for lectures or work in the Bodleian; he had plans now for establishing a school of drawing at the University and gave £5,000 towards it; he would give more later. In April, he was elected an Honorary Fellow of Corpus Christi, a college just behind Christ Church on Merton

Street where he stayed for about three months a year until 1878. He remained on good terms with Corpus throughout his professorship, even after publicly criticizing its *laissez-faire* attitude to the contamination of drink apparently practised in one of its properties. (No one in Corpus noticed the complaint.)

In June, Ruskin lectured controversially on Michelangelo and Tintoretto: he had never had much time for the former (and had always, perhaps, overrated the latter). 'Nearly every existing work by Michael Angelo', he said, 'is an attempt to execute something beyond his power, coupled with a fevered desire that his power may be acknowledged [. . .] Tintoret, on the contrary, works in the consciousness of supreme strength, which cannot be wounded by neglect, and is only to be thwarted by time and space'.[16] The University authorities, proud of their distinguished collection of Michelangelo drawings in the Ashmolean, were affronted.

In July, Ruskin took a holiday in Matlock. This was the occasion of what may have been his first mental breakdown, though it may simply have been a severe case of food poisoning. Whatever it was, he was quite quickly better, cared for by Dr Stokes,

Henry Acland, Mrs Cowper (by this time Cowper-Temple) and Joan Severn, an increasingly important figure in his domestic life. But there was no doubt he had been seriously ill. In August Ruskin reached a positive decision: he bought the old, crumbling villa, Brantwood, on the eastern shore of Coniston Water which, when properly repaired and improved, would provide him with a fine home for the remainder of his life. 'Here', he wrote to Norton on 15 September, remembering his own words in 'Of Queens' Gardens', 'I have rocks, streams, fresh air, and, for the first time in my life, the rest of the purposed *home*.'[17]

Great sadness followed at the end of the year when, on 5 December, Margaret Ruskin, whose illness had been a cause for 'heavy alarm'[18] for some time, died. She was ninety-one. Later, Ruskin would tell one of Henry Acland's sons that 'the remainder of my life was virtually wrecked by the loss of her',[19] but in truth his feelings towards her, as for his father, were much more equivocal. In 1875, in *Fors*, he would start discussing his own upbringing and publicly mulling over his complicated feelings for his two strong-minded parents, trying to be faithful to their love and to 'esteem the main blessings of my childhood' but also counting 'the equally dominant calamities'.[20]

The early months of 1872 saw Ruskin mostly in Oxford, giving the lectures that would be published that year as *The Eagle's Nest*. These were about the moral responsibilities of science in relation to art: in the 'new [Oxford] schools of science', he warned, students 'learn the power of machinery and of physical elements, but not that of the soul'.[21] The shortcomings of modern empirical science, heartless and soulless, would become an increasing preoccupation. The lectures over, Ruskin and a party of friends left for the Continent, passing through Rome ('more repulsive to me than ever')[22] and eventually reaching Venice at the end of June, where he once more threw himself into the art of Carpaccio.

Ruskin described Carpaccio's *Dream of St Ursula* – a particularly important painting for him – in great detail in *Fors* for August 1872 (written in July). He compared the 'evident delight' of Ursula and her 'Royal power over herself'[23] with two American girls he had seen on the train to Verona, who, 'By infinite self-indulgence [. . .] had reduced themselves simply to two pieces of white putty that could feel pain'.[24] He was probably thinking of Rose.

When Ruskin was back in Coniston in September, Rose was again ill and seriously disturbed. Their relationship, if it could be described as such, had continued in cycles of hope and despair during the past few years, mostly through correspondence and messages passed by sympathetic friends. Ruskin had grown increasingly critical of her, but she still exercised a frightening influence on his moods and well-being. He immersed himself in more distracting work during the autumn: preparing lectures, writing *Fors*, sorting out the gardens at Brantwood. In November and December he was in Oxford delivering the lectures on engraving, which would become part of *Ariadne Florentina*. He had been a practical engraver and collector of engravings for a long time. It was, he said in *Ariadne*, the 'first of the arts', and he concentrated on the 'greatest Florentine master of engraving', Sandro Botticelli, and on 'the greatest master of the German', Hans Holbein.[25] Despite the problems with Rose, he was in a positive frame of mind in the winter, and his diary entry for the last day of 1872 was buoyant: 'Intensely dark and rainy morning; but I, on the whole, victorious, and ready for new work'.[26]

Much of 1873 was spent at Brantwood: Ruskin's diary is full of comments on the weather and the beauties of nature around him. In March he was lecturing at Oxford, where he gave the first of the ornithological series he would publish later as *Love's Meinie*, one of his three science books in which he insisted that the study of nature should be a reverent and moral activity. *Love's Meinie* continued his criticism of the 'vile industries and vicious curiosities'[27] of modern, professional science which he had begun in *The Eagle's Nest*. On 10 April 1873, Ruskin recorded in his diary the twenty-fifth anniversary of his disastrous marriage with an ironic biblical quotation: 'Maundy Thursday: *Dies mandati*. The Day of Mandate: that ye love one another.'[28]

Oxford work continued at the end of 1873 with the beginning of the lecture series which would be published as *Val d'Arno*, on Tuscan art. But Ruskin was miserable and depressed, writing plaintively to Carlyle that 'I have not the least pleasure in my work any more', and, musing on his bereavement, that 'the loss of my mother [. . .] leaves me without any root, or, in the depth of the word, any home'.[29]

Problems with Rose continued too: by February 1874, her physical and mental condition had again seriously deteriorated. She was appearing in many of Ruskin's dreams, some of them overtly sexual. In his extraordinary self-portrait, probably dated 1873, the devastating consequences of so many years of anxiety are recorded in the half-shadowed, care-worn face.

One of Ruskin's memorable practical schemes of education was begun in the spring of 1874 when he encouraged his Oxford undergraduates to help construct a road between North and South Hinksey, just outside Oxford. It would teach them the value of useful, properly directed muscular work, he said. The scheme prompted both admiration and amusement, but it ultimately failed to create a good route, as the land was liable to flooding. By April, Ruskin was abroad, travelling to Rome, working in the Sistine Chapel on Botticelli, then in Assisi, where he studied Giotto and Cimabue, and stayed in the Sacristan's cell. On 'the whole,' he wrote to Charles Eliot Norton on 19 June, 'I am greatly disappointed with Giotto, on close study − and on the contrary, altogether amazed at the power of Cimabue'.[30] Cimabue filled Ruskin with wonder −

in the lower church at Assisi, he wrote that Cimabue had painted 'the sublimest Mater Dolorosa [. . .] in the Italian schools'.[31]

Back at Oxford for the Michaelmas term, Ruskin delivered lectures later to be published as part of *Deucalion*, the second of his science books, which, he thought, would comprise an 'absolutely trustworthy' guide to the important facts of geology.[32] Like all his science books, he came presently to envisage *Deucalion*, named after the Noah of Greek myth, as a textbook for the schools planned for the Guild of St George. Lecturing on ornithology and geology, as well as on landscape painting and engraving, discussing politics and economics, encouraging practical road building and trying to teach the elements of drawing, Ruskin's work as Slade Professor exemplified his conviction that 'The teaching of Art [. . .] is the teaching of all things'.[33]

If Oxford work was relatively productive for Ruskin, his private life at the end of 1874 and the beginning of 1875 was entering yet another troubled stage. He recorded in his diary many gloomy statements about the weather: it served as a symbol of his own cloudy emotional life. In

February 1875, he was feeling overwhelmed with work – 'Greatly oppressed by impossibility of doing what I plan, and by failing strength'[34] – and writing to Norton that 'The deadliest of all things to me is my loss of faith in nature.'[35] On 28 May came news of the long-awaited devastation: Rose, who had been ill for so long, had died on 25 May at 7.00 in the morning, before her parents could reach her. 'I've just heard', he wrote to Susan Beever, a friend, 'that my poor little Rose is gone where the hawthorn blossoms go'.[36] Her idealized presence would now increase in Ruskin's mind until the end.

Depression persisted sporadically throughout 1875, and Ruskin continued to draw parallels between the weather and his own dismal state. In May, he began the series for travellers called *Mornings in Florence*. His preface revealed the extent to which he thought of his role now as serving others. 'It seems to me', he wrote, 'that the real duty involved in my Oxford professorship cannot be completely done by giving lectures in Oxford only, but that I ought also to give what guidance I may to travellers in Italy.'[37] In fulfilling such self-imposed duties, he could find some contentment and sense of purpose absent from other parts of his life.

In November, Ruskin lectured on Reynolds's *Discourses*. Only notes of this remain. In December, an interest in spiritualism was revived at Broadlands, the home of the Cowper-Temples. Ruskin was not the only Victorian intellectual to experiment with spiritualism but he invested more in it than many: he was driven by an urgent desire to communicate with Rose. On 14 December, he learnt from a medium at Broadlands 'the most overwhelming evidence of the other state of the world that has ever come to me'[38] and on 21 December he received, he came later to believe, a real sign from Rose. The belief that she was endeavouring to communicate with him, through whatever means she could, now played a significant role in Ruskin's life.

One consequence of Ruskin's experiences at Broadlands was a revival of some of his religious beliefs: 'I have no *new* faith,' he told Norton in March 1876, 'but am able to get some good out of my old one'.[39] In May, he began to keep a separate diary for his time at Brantwood in which he recorded his increasing sense that the climate was cursed and that the foul weather which he had charted for so long was evidence of England's moral contagion and of divine displeasure with the modern world.

Preoccupation with Carpaccio's *Dream of St Ursula* haunted the last months of 1876 when Ruskin was in Venice. In his obsessive work on the picture, which he had specially moved for him in the Accademia, he began to associate the peaceful figure of Ursula with Rose, and to feel that through Carpaccio Rose had found another way of communicating with him. A number of unexpected coincidences over Christmas, such as the arrival by post of a sprig of vervain from a friend at Kew (vervain is depicted in Carpaccio's picture), further convinced Ruskin that Rose was in touch with him. He felt he had become like Dante receiving revelation from Beatrice.

The beginning of 1877 saw still more work on *St Ursula*, but Ruskin was also writing the third of his science books, *Proserpina*, on botany and flower mythology, as well as further reflections on the history and art of Venice. He published the *Guide to the Principal Pictures in the Academy of Fine Arts at Venice*, and, in May, the first part of his *St Mark's Rest* – 'The history of Venice, written for the help of the few travellers who still care for her monuments'.[40]

Ruskin was writing more simply now, and sometimes aiming his words at children. He was also writing a great deal about Carpaccio.

In June, Ruskin was back in London where he visited the newly opened Grosvenor Gallery, a venue for the artistic avant-garde. Here, he saw some of the Impressionist work of James McNeill Whistler whom, notoriously, he accused in the *Fors* letter of July of 'flinging a pot of paint in the public's face'.[41] Whistler, who would write about the event in *The Gentle Art of Making Enemies*, promptly sued Ruskin for libel. The year 1877 closed with Ruskin's readings from *Modern Painters* at Oxford: 'people say I have never given so useful a course yet', he wrote, tired but content.[42] There were so many people, the door had to be propped open so that those outside could hear. It was encouraging amid so much difficulty.

SIX

'RISING AND FALLING, MIXED WITH THE LIGHTNING', 1879–1900

Ruskin spent Christmas 1877 enjoyably with the Aclands in Oxford, and began the new year in good heart. But another dark shadow would soon overtake him. The Brantwood diary records through February his rapid decline into mental illness, his entries becoming more and more fragmentary, erratic and incoherent. One poignant line from 22 February reads: 'Oh – you dear Blake – and so mad too –'.[1] It was a late premonition of his own insanity which struck him that night: he was found deeply demented the following morning. Ruskin's friends feared for his life; when they saw signs that he might regain physical strength, they were anxious that his sanity would be permanently impaired. But in fact, attended by John Simon, he recovered relatively quickly, writing perhaps his first letter, to Acland, on 16 April: 'I wish I could give you some idea', he told him, 'of the long space of life which seemed to pass, and *was* I do not doubt, exhausted, in that delirium'.[2]

Ruskin was convalescing from this illness through the last months of 1878 and, though he was able to dictate instructions to his defence counsel, did not attend the Whistler libel trial held in November. The painter won the case, but was awarded derisory damages of a farthing, a coin he then always wore on his watch chain. The trial produced some interesting discussion about the public utility of art at a time when the Aesthetic Movement, with its faith in *l'art pour l'art*, was increasingly prominent. But there was an air of fatuousness over the proceedings.

Gradually, Ruskin eased himself back into work; he added to *Proserpina* and *Deucalion* during the course of 1879, read Plato, prepared a 'Traveller's Edition' of *The Stones of Venice*. He also studied the life of Herbert Edwardes, the British commander in the Second Sikh War in 1849, whom Ruskin, searching for a model of ideal masculine behaviour in the modern world, would later commemorate in *A Knight's Faith* (1885). His correspondence revived too. But following the delirium his creativity seemed weakened, and only infrequently could he write with the same power that he had in the past. He would often content himself now with editing, translating and revising rather than with new work.

However, in 1880, *Fiction, Fair and Foul* came out serially, in which Ruskin discussed Scott, Byron and Wordsworth. He lamented the 'foul' fiction which was being produced in the modern city, a place of monotony 'where every emotion intended to be derived by men from the sight of nature, or the sense of art, is forbidden forever'.[3] The first portion of *The Bible of Amiens* was also published. Here, Ruskin adopted the role of travel guide, imagining himself showing two children around Amiens and retelling the legends of the city, especially those of St Martin. All great art is praise, Ruskin had often said throughout his life: 'So is all faithful History',[4] he added in the Preface to *The Bible of Amiens*, and endeavoured, by narrating the story of the city, to communicate and commend to younger readers the noble and faithful values he believed had distinguished the Gothic age.

But Ruskin felt at this period that he was on borrowed time, and in his diary for 1880 he recorded many feelings of uncertainty and depression; he was also still watching the weather carefully, continuing to link the gloomy skies with his own melancholy and with his sense that England was under divine judgment. He mused also on efforts he thought made by Rose to communicate with him from another world. On her birthday, 3 January 1880, he opened his Bible to find the passage: 'We know that we have passed from death unto life'.[5] This, he felt, was a comfort sent directly from her.

'Could not have a sadder morning for the birthday', Ruskin noted in his diary exactly one year later, on 3 January 1881: 'Read entry for last year, but am much more dead, myself, in this one.'[6] Time and sickness were taking their toll. Further mental illness, 'terrific delirium' he called it when he recovered,[7] followed in March 1881, and left him able to complete only a modest amount of writing in the remainder of the year (such as a *Master's*

Report for the Guild, and some more of *The Bible of Amiens*). He did manage, also, to renew some of his correspondence, and wrote in particular a number of letters to the Revd John Pincher Faunthorpe, a Ruskin disciple and Principal of Whitelands College, London, whom he had known for some time. Faunthorpe's work as head of a teacher training college for women interested Ruskin greatly, and he supported Whitelands as much as he could, including with gifts of books. He also suggested the idea of the Whitelands May Queen ceremony, which continues to this day, now supported by the Guild of St George. Faunthorpe in due course compiled an *Index to Fors Clavigera* in 1887. But Ruskin thought it hopelessly inadequate. Overall, however, 1881 was a painful year. Ruskin was gradually being broken into pieces.

In March 1882, after a brief period of good work in London in February, Ruskin had yet another serious attack of mental illness, presaged, as was now the pattern, by vivid and disturbing dreams, and eccentric, erratic and frightening behaviour. When insane, Ruskin could be uncontrollable, delirious, violent. A viciously torn book survives today at the University of Texas at Austin as testimony to this. But by April, he was regaining a little of his health; he set about quietly writing some music and continued work on a plan, begun in 1875, to develop a small museum in Sheffield, part of his intention to extend the opportunities for working-class education.

In August, under instruction from his doctor, Ruskin went on a tour to the Continent, in the company of W.G. Collingwood, his secretary and, later, biographer, together with a valet. He was in a persistently retrospective mood during this excursion, remembering past visits. At Champagnole, he wrote in his diary: 'I never thought to date from this dear place more; and I am here in – for my age – very perfect health'.[8] At Sallanches, he was 'never [. . .] happier in seeing the Alps once more',[9] but at Pisa he reflected: 'Here once more, where I began all my true work in 1845. Thirty seven full years of it: how much in vain!'[10] Back in London by December, he was continuing to think of the weather as a 'plague', even having 'dreams of darkness and storm'.[11] It was as if he was seeing the world as a swirling Turner painting.

At the beginning of the new year, Ruskin worked on revising a reissue of *Modern Painters* II, pointing out how his own earlier opinions had been distorted by the narrowness of his Evangelical creed. Re-elected Slade Professor at Oxford in January, he resumed lecturing duties in March, giving the first of a series on D.G. Rossetti and Holman Hunt, which were eventually published as part of *The Art of England*. Kate Greenaway, the children's book illustrator, was his guest at Brantwood from April to May: Ruskin praised her work extravagantly. It was a sad sign of his gradual decline that the rhetorical powers which once brought to life the work of Titian, Turner and Fra Angelico now effused over such quaint pictures. Norton came later and found Ruskin lonely and depressed.

But Ruskin could sometimes be roused to unexpected energy. In the lectures on *The Storm-Cloud of the Nineteenth Century*, delivered in February 1884, Ruskin gave his private depression powerful prophetic shape in one of his most highly charged statements about the modern world. *The Storm-Cloud* grew from what he had been thinking about and recording in his diary for many years: the dire portents found in the weather. England was afflicted with a 'plague-wind' and a 'plague-cloud' which blanched the sun, he said, and the meaning was clear: 'Remember, for the last twenty years, England, and all foreign nations, either tempting her, or following her, have blasphemed the name of God deliberately and openly [. . .] Of states in such moral gloom every seer of old predicted the physical gloom, saying, "The light shall be darkened in the heavens thereof, and the stars shall withdraw their shining." '[12] England was under curse, and her blighted weather proved it.

In May, Ruskin returned to Brantwood, pursued still by 'Pestiferous rain and plague wind and unbroken fog'.[13] He spent time entertaining, walking in the countryside and doing some work on *Fors*. But his companions, especially Joan Severn, were ever fearful of returning insanity. He was in Oxford in October to lecture and to hear services 'in my own Cathedral'.[14] But his diary at the end of the year was full of complaints of illness and languor. He found exertion dangerous, and wanted, he wrote, 'never [to] stir out of quiet work more'.[15]

Quiet work, punctuated by bouts of severe insanity or periods that looked as if they might become such, characterized the remaining years of Ruskin's working life. In March 1885, he resigned from the Slade Professorship, partly because he no

longer felt strong enough to continue the duties he
had taken so seriously, and partly because he was
incensed by the University's commitment to
vivisection. 'I cannot lecture in the next room to a
shrieking cat', he wrote, '– nor address myself to
the men who have been – there's no word for it'.[16]
He was deeply 'in a passion'[17] over Acland's
determined support of vivisection too. Acland's
involvement was an irony in Ruskin's resignation of
the professorship; the fact that it was in the
University museum complex – long ago intended
by Ruskin as the place of the reverent study of
nature – that vivisection was practised was another.
Ruskin felt doubly betrayed.

Between periods of illness, Ruskin managed
occasional writing. His chief accomplishment,
during periods of lucidity and strength, was the
composition of *Praeterita* – the title means 'Of past
things' – a sudden, final and remarkable rekindling
of his literary powers. He began it in 1885, writing
in the Preface in what was once his own nursery at
Herne Hill (now the home of Joan Severn and her
husband Arthur when they were not at Brantwood):
it was never finished. *Praeterita*, one of the most
eloquent and accessible of all Victorian

autobiographies, is rich with elegy, and with the kind of Fra Angelico-like serenity Ruskin himself had once described as an attribute of great religious art. Passing 'in total silence things which I have no pleasure in reviewing,'[18] Ruskin concentrated on his childhood and the beginnings of all his life's enthusiasms: the Alps, geology, Turner, Tintoretto, Venetian history, the Gothic. He tried to balance his thoughts about his parents, repeating earlier reflections from *Fors*, and about Oxford, and to pay tribute to his friends. He said nothing of his marriage.

The last chapter, dated from Brantwood, 19 June 1889, was hastily added as Ruskin feared he would soon have no more strength to write: entitled 'Joanna's Care', it was an offering of thanks to Joan Severn for her friendship and continued nursing. It was almost the last thing Ruskin wrote. His doctors, looking desperately for a remedy for physical and mental exhaustion, had prescribed a continental journey from the summer of 1888, and he had found some fragile happiness walking among the places he had long loved. At Sallanches, he wrote 'Thank God for all my life to come for letting me see such loveliness again.'[19] But the last two entries in his diary for 1888 said it all: at Bassano on 30 September, he wrote, 'I don't know what is going to become of me.'[20] On 10 October, at Venice, once for him the paradise of cities, he added, 'And still less here. . .'.[21] He collapsed distraught in Paris and was taken home by Joan.

Ruskin managed to finish those final pages of *Praeterita* but, wracked by illness, he did hardly anything else in 1889. Recurrent periods of severe illness had left him seriously weakened; by the end of the year, his debilitated condition became permanent. His life, to all intents and purposes, was over. During the course of the remaining eleven years at Brantwood, the frail, troubled man was hardly able to lift a pen and spoke only with difficulty. Brantwood life was orderly, and the Severns carefully guarded – some would say too carefully – the man known by those around him simply as 'the Professor' from the outside world. He saw visitors very infrequently: Acland came and was photographed with his old friend by his daughter; Holman Hunt was there too. Bands occasionally played for him on the lawns of Brantwood, he listened to the newspapers read aloud, he interested himself in a collection to relieve those injured in the

Boer War, he heard the occasional passages from Walter Scott and other novelists and he looked over Arthur Severn's paintings and studies. When Coniston Water froze over, the Brantwood party had their photograph taken on the ice. Ruskin stared out of it, an empty shell.

Though the decline was long, the end itself came with suddenness. On the morning of 18 January 1900, Joan read Edna Lyell's *In the Golden Days* to him, but his throat was irritable and he felt pain 'all over'.[22] He was put to bed by Baxter, his servant, and Joan sang a favourite song, 'Summer Slumber'. That evening he seemed a little recovered and enjoyed a dinner of sole, pheasant and champagne, waking the following morning feeling quite well. But on Saturday 20 January, there was suddenly a great change for the worse: Ruskin had influenza and the doctor was gravely alarmed. Gradually and peacefully, Ruskin sank into unconsciousness and, at 2.00 p.m., he died. Westminster Abbey, his friends were told, was open to him. But, following his own wishes, Ruskin was buried across the water from Brantwood in the quiet churchyard of Coniston.

Eleven years previously, Ruskin's literary work, which had been so much more successful than his life, had closed almost literally with these last, eloquent words about Siena from *Praeterita*:

> Fonte Branda I last saw with Charles Norton, under the same arches where Dante saw it. We drank of it together, and walked together that evening on the hills above, where the fireflies among the scented thickets shone fitfully in the still undarkened air. *How* they shone! moving like fine-broken starlight through the purple leaves. How they shone! through the sunset that faded into thunderous night as I entered Siena three days before, the white edges of the mountainous clouds still lighted from the west, and the openly golden sky calm behind the Gate of Siena's heart, with its still golden words, '*Cor magis tibi Sena pandit*,' and the fireflies everywhere in sky and cloud rising and falling, mixed with the lightning, and more intense than the stars.[23]

They may stand as an epitaph for England's greatest art critic and one of Victorian England's most remarkable minds.

NOTES

CHAPTER ONE

1. E.T. Cook and Alexander Wedderburn (eds), *The Library Edition of The Complete Works of John Ruskin* (39 vols, London, Allen, 1903–12), 9.17. Hereafter cited by volume number and page only.

2. See John Ruskin, *Iteriad or Three Weeks Among the Lakes*, ed. James S. Dearden (Newcastle-upon-Tyne, Graham, 1969).

3. James S. Dearden (ed.), *A Tour to the Lakes in Cumberland: John Ruskin's Diary for 1830* (Aldershot, Scolar, 1990), pp. 57–60.

4. Van Akin Burd (ed.), *The Ruskin Family Letters: The Correspondence of John James Ruskin, His Wife, and Their Son, John 1801–1843* (2 vols, Ithaca and London, Cornell University Press, 1973), I. 278.

5. 35.116.

6. Akin Burd (ed.), *Ruskin Family Letters*, I. 295.

7. Ibid., I.7.

8. Ibid., I.9.

9. Joan Evans and J.H. Whitehouse (eds), *The Diaries of John Ruskin* (3 vols, continuous pagination, Oxford, Clarendon, 1956–9), p. 183. Hereafter *D*.

10. 35.51.

11. 1.310.

12. Akin Burd (ed.), *Ruskin Family Letters*, II. 718.

13. 35.311.

14. 35.314.

15. Ibid.

16. Quoted in Timothy Hilton, *John Ruskin: The Early Years 1819–1859* (New Haven, Yale University Press, 1985), p. 39.

17. 3.252.

18. Quoted in Hilton, *John Ruskin: The Early Years*, p. 73.

19. J.L. Bradley (ed.), *Ruskin: The Critical Heritage* (London, Routledge and Kegan Paul, 1984), p. 64.

20. Bradley (ed.), *Critical Heritage*, p. 76.

21. Bradley (ed.), *Critical Heritage*, p. 64.

22. Bradley (ed.), *Critical Heritage*, p. 37.

CHAPTER TWO

1. 26.219.

2. *D*, p. 318.

3. 4.347.

4. 4.122n.

5. Harold I. Shapiro (ed.), *Ruskin in Italy: Letters to His Parents 1845* (Oxford, Clarendon Press, 1972), p. 67.

6. Shapiro (ed.), *Ruskin in Italy*, p. 203.

7. Shapiro (ed.), *Ruskin in Italy*, pp. 200–1.

8. Shapiro (ed.), *Ruskin in Italy*, p. 211.

9. 35.372.

10. 4.228.

11. 4.274.

12. Bradley (ed.), *Critical Heritage*, p. 87.

13. *D*, p. 254.

14. Letter from Effie, 4 July 1848, in William James (ed.), *The Order of Release* (London, Murray, 1948), p. 115.

15. Letter of 20 July 1848 in James (ed.), *The Order of Release*, p. 118.

16. Francis O'Gorman, 'Ruskin and Walter Lucas Brown: Two New Letters', *Notes & Queries* 46 (1999), p. 58.

17. *D*, p. 383.

18. *D*, p. 421.

19. Ibid.

20. *D*, p. 455.

21. Quoted in Hilton, *John Ruskin: The Early Years*, p. 144.

22. *D*, p. 465.

23. *D*, p. 468.

24. 9.17.

25. 11.148.

26. Quoted in Fiona McCarthy, *William Morris: A Life for Our Time* (London, Faber, 1994), p. 69.

27. J.L. Bradley (ed.), *Ruskin's Letters from Venice 1851–1852* (New

Notes

Haven, Yale University Press, 1955), p. 111. Turner died on 19 December.

28. Bradley, *Ruskin's Letters from Venice*, p. 114. Italic original.

29. 36.115.

30. 24.22.

31. *D*, p. 498.

CHAPTER THREE

1. 5.262.

2. 5.69.

3. 6.416.

4. 6.418.

5. Ibid.

6. 13.170–1.

7. 15.27.

8. [Anon.], *Exhibition of Art Treasures of the United Kingdom, Manchester 1857: Report of the Executive Committee* (Manchester, Simms, 1859), p. 28.

9. Quoted in Hilton, *John Ruskin: The Early Years*, p. 247. Letter of 19 February 1858.

10. Bradley (ed.), *Critical Heritage*, p. 205.

11. Quoted in John Hayman (ed.), *John Ruskin: Letters from the Continent 1858* (Toronto, Toronto University Press, 1982), p. [xiii].

12. Hayman (ed.), *Letters from the Continent*, p. 52.

13. 7.5.

14. 7.293.

15. *D*, p. 537.

16. 29.89.

17. Van Akin Burd (ed.), *John Ruskin and Rose La Touche: Her Unpublished Diaries of 1861 and 1867* (Oxford, Clarendon Press, 1979), p. 43.

18. Quoted in Akin Burd (ed.), *The Winnington Letters: John Ruskin's Correspondence with Margaret Alexis Bell and the Children at Winnington Hall* (London, Allen and Unwin, 1969), p. 33.

19. Quoted in Akin Burd (ed.), *The Winnington Letters*, p. 33.

20. Akin Burd (ed.), *The Winnington Letters*, p. 105.

21. Quoted in Michael W. Brooks, *John Ruskin and Victorian Architecture* (London, Thames and Hudson, 1989), p. 126.

22. Brooks, *John Ruskin and Victorian Architecture*, p. 127.

23. 16.lii.n.

24. Robert Hewison, *Ruskin and Oxford:The Art of Education* (Oxford, Clarendon Press, 1996), p. 13.

25. 16.251.

26. See G.H. Fleming, *John Everett Millais: A Biography* (London, Constable, 1998).

CHAPTER FOUR

1. E.T. Cook, *The Life of John Ruskin* (2 vols, London, Allen, 1912), II.2.

2. 7.207.

3. 7.455.

4. 17.17.

5. Bradley (ed.), *Critical Heritage*, p. 277.

6. Bradley (ed.), *Critical Heritage*, p. 278.

7. Bradley (ed.), *Critical Heritage*, p. 279.

8. 17.105.

9. Akin Burd (ed.), *The Winnington Letters*, p. 278.

10. Akin Burd (ed.), *The Winnington Letters*, p. 281.

11. 36.356.

12. 36.381.

13. J.L. Bradley (ed.), *The Letters of John Ruskin to Lord and Lady Mount-Temple* (Ohio State University Press, 1964), p. 89.

14. 36.415.

15. 17.131.

16. Akin Burd (ed.), *TheWinnington Letters*, p. 420.

17. 36.461.

18. 36. 469.

19. 36.471.

20. 18.433.

21. 18.458.

22. 18.110.

23. 18.121.

24. 18.122.

25. 19.58.

26. 18.346.

Notes

27. Bradley (ed.), *The Letters of John Ruskin to Lord and Lady Mount-Temple*, p. 52.

28. *D*, p. 609.

29. 17.lxxix.

30. 17.313.

31. 17.319.

32. *D*, p. 647.

33. John Dixon Hunt, *The Wider Sea: A Life of John Ruskin* (London, Dent, 1982), p. 321.

CHAPTER FIVE

1. *D*, p. 664.

2. 19.296.

3. *D*, p. 669.

4. *D*, p. 668.

5. Quoted in Dixon Hunt, *The Wider Sea*, p. 324.

6. *D*, p. 679.

7. Bradley (ed.), *The Letters of John Ruskin to Lord and Lady Mount-Temple*, p. 230.

8. *D*, p. 691.

9. Akin Burd (ed.), *John Ruskin and Rose La Touche*, p. 120.

10. Ibid.

11. 20.39. Italic original.

12. 20.42.

13. 20.13.

14. Akin Burd (ed.), *John Ruskin and Rose La Touche*, p. 122.

15. Quoted in Peter Wardle and Cedric Quayle, *Ruskin and Bewdley* (St Alban's, Brentham, 1989), p. 24.

16. 22.87.

17. 37.35. Italic original.

18. *D*, p. 714.

19. Francis O'Gorman, 'Ruskin and the Aclands: Further Letters', *Bodleian Library Record* XVI (1997), 184.

20. 28.350.

21. 22.285.

22. *D*, p. 725.

23. 27.344.

24. 27.345–6.

25. 22.305.

26. *D*, p. 734.

27. 25.56.

28. *D*, p. 742.

29. 37.72.

30. 37.112.

31. 37.114.

32. 26.197.

33. 29.86.

34. *D*, p. 837.

35. 37.161.

36. Akin Burd (ed.), *John Ruskin and Rose La Touche*, p. 133.

37. 23.293.

38. *D*, p. 876.

39. 37.194. Italic original.

40. The subtitle.

41. 29.160.

42. 37.231.

CHAPTER SIX

1. Helen Gill Viljoen (ed.), *The Brantwood Diary of John Ruskin* (New Haven, Yale University Press, 1971), p. 101. Hereafter *BD*.

2. O'Gorman, 'Ruskin and the Aclands', 183.

3. 34.272.

4. 33.23.

5. *BD*, p. [215].

6. *BD*, p. [263].

7. *BD*, p. 268.

8. *D*, p. 1021.

9. *D*, p. 1023.

10. *D*, p. 1028.

11. *D*, p. 1044.

12. 34.40–1.

13. *D*, p. 1065.

14. *D*, p. 1084.

15. *D*, p. 1089.

Notes

16. Quoted in Hewison, *Ruskin and Oxford*, p. 42.
17. *D*, p. 1102.
18. 35.11.
19. *D*, p. 1148.
20. *D*, p. 1150.
21. Ibid.
22. This and other details from the *Barrow News*, 27 January 1900, 3.
23. 35.561–2. The inscription means 'More than her gates, Siena opens her heart to you'.

...of our complete list or details of other Sutton titles, please
...ma Leitch at Sutton Publishing Limited, Phoenix Mill,
...oud, Gloucestershire, GL5 2BU

BIBLIOGRAPHY

Place of publication is London unless stated otherwise.

EDITION

Cook, E.T. and Wedderburn, Alexander (eds). *The Library Edition of The Complete Works of John Ruskin*, 39 vols, Allen, 1903–12. Also now available from Cambridge University Press on CD-ROM (1996)

DIARIES

Dearden, James S. (ed.). *A Tour to the Lakes in Cumberland: John Ruskin's Diary for 1830*, Aldershot, Scolar, 1990

Evans, Joan and Whitehouse, J.H. (eds). *The Diaries of John Ruskin*, 3 vols, Oxford, Clarendon Press, 1956–9. This is a selected edition, with important omissions.

Viljoen, Helen Gill (ed.). *The Brantwood Diary of John Ruskin*, New Haven, Yale University Press, 1971

LETTERS

Significant collections of letters from such a prolific correspondent include:

Akin Burd, Van (ed.). *The Ruskin Family Letters: The Correspondence of John James Ruskin, His Wife, and Their Son, John 1801–1843*, 2 vols, Ithaca, Cornell University Press, 1973

——. *The Winnington Letters: John Ruskin's Correspondence with Margaret Alexis Bell and the Children at Winnington Hall*, Allen and Unwin, 1969

Bradley, J.L. (ed.). *Ruskin's Letters from Venice 1851–1852*, New Haven, Yale University Press, 1955

Shapiro, Harold I. (ed.). *Ruskin in Italy: Letters to His Parents 1845*, Oxford, Clarendon Press, 1972

ART

Penny, Nicholas. *Ruskin's Drawings*, Oxford, Phaidon, 1989

Walton, Paul. *The Drawings of John Ruskin*, Oxford, Clarendon Press, 1972

BIOGRAPHY AND BIOGRAPHICAL RELATED

Akin Burd, Van (ed.). *John Ruskin and Rose La Touche: Her Unpublished Diaries of 1861 and 1867*, Oxford, Clarendon Press, 1979

Dearden, James S. *Facets of Ruskin: Some Sesquicentennial Studies*, Skilton, 1970

Dixon Hunt, John. *The Wider Sea: A Life of John Ruskin*, Dent, 1982

Hilton, Timothy. *John Ruskin: The Early Years 1819–1859*, New Haven, Yale University Press, 1985. The first of a projected, still incomplete, 2-volume life.

Leon, Derrick. *Ruskin: The Great Victorian*, Routledge and Kegan Paul, 1949

Lutyens, Mary. *Effie in Venice*, Murray, 1965

Viljoen, Helen Gill. *Ruskin's Scottish Heritage*, Urbana, University of Illinois Press, 1956. On Ruskin's ancestors.

Birch, Dinah. *Ruskin's Myths,*

——. 'Ruskin's "Womanl (1988), 308–24

——. (ed.). *Ruskin and th* Clarendon Press, 1999

Brooks, Michael W. *John* Thames and Hudson, 1989

Clegg, Jeanne. *Ruskin and Ve*

Dixon Hunt, John and Ho *Polygon: Essays on the Imagin* Manchester University Pres

Fitch, Raymond E. *The Pc Ruskin*, Ohio University Pre

Hewison, Robert. *John Rusk* and Hudson, 1976

——. (ed.). *New Approc* Routledge and Kegan Paul,

Landow, George P. *The Aes Ruskin*, Princeton, Princeto

Sawyer, Paul. *Ruskin's Poetic Works*, Ithaca, Cornell Unive

Sherburne, James Clark. *Abundance: A Study in Social* MA, Harvard University Pr

Wheeler, Michael. *Ruskin* University Press, 1999

POCKET BIOGRAPHIES

For a copy of our complete list or details of other Sutton titles, please contact Emma Leitch at Sutton Publishing Limited, Phoenix Mill, Thrupp, Stroud, Gloucestershire, GL5 2BU

POCKET BIOGRAPHIES

FORTHCOMING

Joseph Stalin
Harold Shukman

Juan and Eva Perón
Clive Foss

Queen Victoria
Elizabeth Longford

Lord Byron
Catherine Peters

Anthony Trollope
Graham Handley

For a copy of our complete list or details of other Sutton titles, please contact Emma Leitch at Sutton Publishing Limited, Phoenix Mill, Thrupp, Stroud, Gloucestershire, GL5 2BU